PN Review 228

Volume 42, Number 4

March–April 2016

Poems

Reports

Features

Reviews

Editorial

In 2008, at the launch of his *Collected Poems*, I presented Christopher Middleton with an early copy of the 720-page tome. He took it with one hand and with the other mischievously handed me the manuscript of his *next* collection. *Collected Poems* was not the definitive monument, not by a long chalk. In 2014 Carcanet repeated the monumental gesture with a *Collected Later Poems* (440 pages). Again, there was more to come. Sheep Meadow Press published *Nobody's Ezekiel* (2015), 48 further pages. Among his papers, another book or pamphlet no doubt crouches, preparing to leap out at us. He has always been a poet of surprises. I am reluctant to commit him to the preterite, though in November 2015 he was reported to have died in Austin, Texas, in his ninetieth year.

The first of his almost eighty prose and verse contributions to this magazine was the poem 'Anasphere: le Torse Antique' (*Poetry Nation*, 1975). In those days *PNR*, as *Poetry Nation*, appeared twice a year in hardback. Even then, in an issue featuring among others Donald Davie, C. H. Sisson, Octavio Paz, James Atlas and Calvin Bedient, he was the odd man (the contributors were almost all men) out. His four-part poem, with a transliterated Japanese epigraph, a free-verse movement progressing towards fragmentation, an alertness to violence, a sense of travelling witness, evokes a now beloved, now minatory, always changing 'you'.

When he submitted work for book publication at Carcanet in 1974, I took soundings from poets I thought might be attuned to his writing. They urged me not to publish it. It was eccentric, Germanic, too experimental. I kept re-reading *The Lonely Suppers of W. V. Balloon* (1975) and could not bring myself to say no. Forty years and eighteen Carcanet books later, his *oeuvre*, almost nineteenth-century in scale, amounts in formal and thematic diversity to a whole restless literature in itself, enhanced by essays, fictions and translations. It stands always at an oblique angle to his age and resists assimilation into 'movements' with which it shares passing affinities.

In Austin he was appointed Professor in Germanic Languages and Literature in 1966, retiring in 1998, but remaining in Austin, with forays to Europe and Asia Minor. Exile was deliberate. He knew England and its cultural habits well (born in Cornwall, raised in Cambridge, four years' service in the RAF, university at Oxford) and chose to regard them from a healthy distance, where he did not have to fight for oxygen.

In his finest (two-part) essay, 'Notes on the Viking Prow' (*PNR* 10, 16; 1979, 1980), he writes,

To recapture poetic reality in a tottering world, we may have to revise, once more, the idea of a poem as an expression of the 'contents' of a subjectivity. Some poems, at least, and some types of poetic language, constitute structures of a singularly radiant kind, where 'self-expression' has undergone a profound change of function. We experience these structures, if not as revelations of being, then as apertures upon being. We experience them as we experience nothing else.

His argument is hortatory, pulling back the corner on creative possibilities which look new but are in fact the *fons et origo*.

If poets have the subtlety and tenacity to take his arguments on board, even if consciously to reject them, it will mark the beginning of a change in the creative environment. There is a severity in Middleton, the trained philologist, scholar and translator, the luminous critic, and there is a tonic playfulness. He emphasises how important *irrelevance* is in education, resisting the pressure of educators to assign texts to which students can 'relate'. The *other* takes us onward from where we are, even when that *other* is in the past. The apparently relevant can arrest and retard.

In his essay 'On the Apotropaic Element in Poetry' (*PNR* 143, 2002) he writes of the 'second intention' in the language of poetry. 'About the best poetry, and not only the best, there floats an atmosphere of infinite suggestion. The poet speaks to us of one thing, but in this one thing there seems to lurk the secret of all [...] which, we feel, would satisfy not only the imagination, but the whole of us.' He quotes the humanist geneticist Albert Jacquard, from his 1994 essay 'Demain dépend de nous' which 'appeals – by synopsis on an exalted level, rather than by empirical scrutiny'. Jacquard suggests that the person is defined by belonging in formal language, is contained in belonging; a belonging consciously experienced sporadically. One place it might be experienced is in liturgy. Another, in a secular age, is in a poem. This is not to suggest the achieved arts as a surrogate metaphysics but to affirm that, as always, they are places not of differentiation but of communion, a communion that need not have transcendent implications beyond the transcending of the isolated individual, who becomes a person in that transcendence.

A mastery of language, the element of containment and expression, enhances belonging. 'So the arts arrive like guardian angels to pick out from the crowd not anybody, not somebody, but everybody. Then everybody reconfigures as a group of persons [...]. Art serves no purpose here but an illumination of being, if not the fullness of being, then a spending and storage of consciousness [...]' His conclusion epitomises his art and teaching and challenges an age in which poetry is made instrumental: good poems

[...] do remain purposeless, as play – radiant ludic phenomena, singular even as they enter history and stay there, corpuscles that no wave can digest; and that, notwithstanding, certain works of art – variously paradoxical as they are – do, in a sense, purpose something. Or no. I should rephrase this: Independently of its author, a work of verbal art, if animated by a certain element, is primed to avert evil. Intangible, indefinable as any *purpose* may be, that work of art is apotropaic.

News & Notes

Jaan Kaplinski

The Estonian writer and philosopher Jaan Kaplinski has been awarded the 2016 European Prize for Literature. Born in Tartu in 1941, Kaplinski studied linguistics at Tartu University and started his poetic life under the influence of Shelley and Lermontov, from which he recovered to write his distinctive verse, and to translate texts from various languages into Estonian. His works in English include the novel *The Same River* (Peter Owen), poetry translations with Harvill (London), Laurel Press (Canada), and a *Selected Poems* (2011) from Bloodaxe which has published his poetry for more than a dozen years.

T.S. Eliot Prize

Sarah Howe, who has contributed poems and an essay on Jorie Graham to *PN Review*, was awarded the 2016 T.S. Eliot Prize in January. Sarah's *Loop of Jade* was the first ever début collection to win, from a shortlist that included Mark Doty, Tracey Herd, Selima Hill, Tim Liardet, Les Murray, Sean O'Brien, Don Paterson, Rebecca Perry and Claudia Rankine. Sarah held the Harper-Wood Studentship at St John's College, Cambridge in 2012. She was born in Hong Kong to a Chinese mother and an English father and moved to England when she was nine. She used the Harper-Wood to revisit her birthplace and consider her mixed heritage. The judges' decision was unexpected and generally welcomed. The chair of the judges, Pascale Petit, praised the book's 'startling exploration of gender and injustice through place and identity, its erudition, and powerful imagery as well as her daring experiment with form'. Sarah also won the 2015 *Sunday Times* Young Writer of the Year Award. She is currently on a writing Fellowship at the Radcliffe Institute, Harvard.

Private Eye portrayed her victory as a plot. Oliver Thring interviewed the poet in the *Sunday Times* and rewarded her candour with slighting asides. 'It is entirely dismissive', the *Guardian* agrees. Thring is not the ideal interviewer for her, impatient with difficulty and with an opportunist's eye, not a reader's ear. The Twittering that followed his piece compelled him to Tweet, 'This gentle interview with a leading young poet has led various deranged poetesses to call me thick, sexist etc.' The ugly side-show to the happy outcome of the Eliot Prize reveals how certain attitudes – to education, gender and race – continue to distort judgment and taint discourse.

Queen's Gold Medal for Poetry

The Queen's Gold Medal for Poetry, 2015, was awarded to Liz Lochhead, Scotland's Makar. The Queen would be well advised to deal gingerly with the author of *Mary Queen of Scots Got Her Head Chopped Off* (1987), a poet of strong political convictions, described by her old friend the Poet Laureate as having brought 'a new kind of poetry performance to the stage' with 'her own feisty, female voice, mixing old Scots with new Scots [...] and she did this with a galvanising spirit and vitality that helped to change the landscape of British poetry.' The BBC made clear the process of selection. The Poet Laureate chairs 'a panel of experts chosen by the Poet Laureate at the time'. The discussions are *in camera*, the membership of the panel not announced.

Pablo Neruda

In late December the streets of Santiago, Chile, witnessed a giant inflatable Pablo Neruda – twenty metres long and four metres high, his enormous face smiling, his hands gesturing – floating above the buildings, leading a colourful parade with more than six hundred participants, with music and recitals to memorialise the life and work of the Nobel laureate. He floated like an overweight figure from a Chagall painting over Recoleta, Independencia and Santiago. The poet's balloon was accompanied by other balloons: an enormous dove, a figurehead, books, conches and butterflies. At fifteen 'stations' – the poet having died shortly after the Pinochet coup toppled Salvador Allende – the procession paused to enact, meditate, sing, dance... At the Municipal Library a sculpture of Neruda was unveiled. The procession ended, appropriately, in the Plaza of Peace, facing the Cementerio General.

Ahmad Zahid Hamidi

In Malaysia, on 5 December, the Deputy Prime Minister Datuk Seri Dr Ahmad Zahid Hamidi closed the sixth Pangkor Poetry and Folk Song Festival in a dinner speech urging poets to produce songs and poems relevant to the young generation. 'Many of those from Generation X', he said, 'do not appreciate' what was on offer. 'We have to read their minds and create something more relevant and futuristic.' He proceeded to read a poem of his own, to 'thunderous applause', the *New Straits Times* says, though the diners were not all from Generation X. Five hundred poets and musicians participated in the Festival, some from as far afield as Indonesia and Singapore.

C.D. Wright (1949–2016)

'I write it, study it, read it, edit it, publish it, teach it... sometimes I weary of it. I could not live without it. Not in this world. Not in my lifetime.' C. (Carolyn) D. Wright died suddenly on 12 January at her home in Rhode Island. She was born in Mountain Home, Arkansas, in 1949, and attended Memphis State University and the University of Arkansas. She wrote more than a dozen books of poems, winning with her 2010 collection *One With Others* (Copper Canyon Press) the Lenore Marshall Poetry Prize, the National Book Critics Circle Award, and was a National Book Award finalist. She was honoured with several awards and fellowships and in 2013 was elected a Chancellor of the Academy of

American Poets. 'It is a function of poetry to locate those zones inside us that would be free,' she said, 'and declare them so.' In 'Our Dust' she wrote,

I was a poet of hummingbird hives along with redhead stepbrothers.
The poet of good walking shoes—a necessity in vernacular parts—and push mowers.

Anne Waldman called Wright 'one of our most fearless writers, possessed with an urgency that pierces through the darkness of our time. [...] Hers is a necessary poetics, on fire with life and passion for what matters.' She is survived by her husband, the poet Forrest Gander, and their son Brecht.

Delmore Schwartz

In *PN Review* 226 we published John Ashbery's 'The Heavy Bear: Delmore Schwartz's Life versus his Poetry'. This essay, the New York publisher New Directions advises us, will 'serve as an introduction to our forthcoming collection *Once and For All: The Best of Delmore Schwartz*'. Meike Chew adds, 'Schwartz's star has really faded over the decades which saddens everyone here at New Directions. He was one of our very first authors. With this collection we hope to reinvigorate his legacy and introduce him to new readers.' More information is available on http://www.ndbooks.com/book/once-and-for-all-the-best-of-delmore-schwartz/.

Francisco Xavier Alarcón (1954–2016)

Francisco Xavier Alarcón, the prolific Chicano author of poetry books for adults and children, died in January. He was born in California, grew up in Guadalajara, Mexico, then returned to attend California State University at Long Beach, taking an MA from Stanford. His poetry is marked by fascination with mythology, the Nahuatl language, Middle American history, and his gay, Latino perspectives. He received the 1984 Chicano Literary Prize, the 1993 PEN Oakland Josephine Miles Award, and a Fred Cody Lifetime Achievement Award from the Bay Area Book Reviewers Association in 2002.

Kazuo Kawamura (1933–2015)

Kazuo Kawamura, Emeritus Professor of English Literature at Kanto Gakuin University in Yokohama, died on 26th November 2015 at the age of 82. He pursued the study of Shelley and Dante life-long and was co-director with colleague William I. Elliott of the Kanto Poetry Center. They founded *Poetry Kanto* and translated some fifty-five collections of the poet Shuntaro Tanikawa, whose *New Selected Poems* were published by Carcanet in October of 2015.

Mangesh Padgaonkar (1929–2015)

The *Times of India* reports the death of Marathi poet Mangesh Padgaonkar. He was eighty-six. He received a state funeral. Best known for his love songs, Padgaonkar collaborated with Vinda Karandikar and Vasant Bapat in the 1960s, making poetry popular among Marathis. The three men read and performed throughout the country, keeping their distance from political and rising bourgeois interests. The establishment mourned his death, however: his was a loved voice. His publisher declared, 'Padgaonkar never believed in penury, which we Indians associate with poets. He was always nattily dressed and loved a glass of whiskey after a reading show.'

Irving Weinman (1937–2015)

contributed by James Sutherland-Smith
On the 26th of October 2015 intellectual life in Britain became significantly poorer following the death of Irving Weinman of a heart attack at the age of seventy-eight. I first met Irving at the old Poetry Society in Earls Court Square where we were both participants in one of the then equivalents of open-mic evenings called Poetry Round and at the rigorous invitation-only Poets' Workshop, the London progeny of the Group which had George MacBeth and Alan Brownjohn, Carol Rumens, James Berry and Judith Kazantzis as members. Irving and I were also habitués of Farida Majid's literary salon in Cadogan Square, which included Fleur Adcock, Gavin Ewart, George MacBeth, Ian Robinson, Andrew Waterman and John Welch among others. Irving and I became close friends and I was often his and his first wife, Zoe's, guest at their palatial apartment in Holland Park. Irving worked as a lecturer in English at Maryland University in Britain teaching American servicemen stationed on bases in Britain.

His parents were well-to-do Romanian Jews who had come to America via Paris before the Second World War. Those of Irving's relatives who remained perished in the death camps. His parents settled in Boston and he grew up in an intellectual liberal household where four languages were commonly spoken, his mother being proficient in no less than seven. After a school education from which he emerged with a gift for science and great skill as a jazz pianist he went to MIT, but after his first degree he took a second degree in literature. He participated in workshops with Anne Sexton and may even have been taught by Robert Lowell, whom he knew well. He was particularly close to Anne Sexton until he left for Europe with Zoe. He continued to study at Trinity College, Dublin before moving to London where he taught and Zoe modelled. They were a fashionable and well-connected couple. So when Rudolf Nureyev defected Irving and Zoe sheltered him in their flat. They may have also played a role in the defection of Natalia Makarova. Irving, a very handsome man, once told me that he'd managed to deflect the inevitable pass from Nureyev without causing offence. Irving and Zoe also gave shelter to the defecting novelist Anatoli Kuznetsov and to Harry Fainlight after his mental breakdown following his love affair with Allen Ginsberg.

From the early 1980s for the following twenty years Irving divided his time between England and Key West with his new partner and later wife, Judith Kazantzis. He wrote fiction, including three detective novels of which the best, *Virgil's Ghost*, is a minor classic. They made him money and were critical successes. There were two further novels which were received less well partly because they never shook off the trappings of the genre in which he had begun. He and Judith were at the centre of a thriving intellectual colony in Key West which included Leonard Bernstein, John Malcolm Brinnin, Harry Mathews, James Merrill and Richard Wilbur. In 1983 he co-founded the Key West Literary Workshop, which is now a major literary event in the United States. In the last decade of his life he and Judith settled in Lewes in Sussex, the home of a number of writers. He produced a guide to writing fiction and at the time of his death was at work on short stories based on his family, a number of which are located in pre-war Romania.

He was a considerate and generous reader of my early work even putting up some of the money to print my first collection of poetry from the Many Press. When I tried to repay him a few months after it was published he refused to accept my money. Later the Many Press published Irving's chapbook, *Storm Warning*, his only collection of poetry although there are two poems in Farida Majid's *Thursday Evening Anthology* which collected poems read at her salon.

His death has deprived Anglophone literature of a great champion and practitioner, a loss made greater by the fact that his modesty about his life and achievements did not alert a publisher into persuading him to write his memoirs.

Aleš Debeljak (1961–2016)

Patrick McGuinness writes from Ljubljana:
The Slovenian poet and cultural critic Aleš Debeljak died on 28 January in a road accident. He was fifty-four. Born in Ljubljana in 1961, he first distinguished himself as a Yugoslav junior judo champion, a sport he abandoned because of injury. He was publishing poetry from the mid-1980s, and studied comparative literature at the university of Ljubljana before pursuing graduate studies in the United States. His first book of poems, with the classic cold war title *Dictionary of Silence*, appeared in 1987, and marked him out as a writer out step with official culture.

He published a further eight books of poems and fourteen books of essays, including the 1994 *Twilight of the Idols: Recollections of a Lost Yugoslavia* (published in 1995 in English by White Pines Press, translated by Michael Biggins). It is a moving, occasionally culturally (but not politically) nostalgic exploration of a shared artistic culture, written as the Yugoslav war raged, and testifies to the breadth of his sympathies at a time when reaching for extremes – of anger or resignation – would have been easier.

He had returned to Slovenia from the United States in 1990, and witnessed the ten-day war of 1991, one of the triggers of the Yugoslav war, when he worked with foreign media covering the clashes between the newly-declared Slovenian republic and the Yugoslav army.

His poetry blends the personal (the voice is always human, unmistakably unified, though always changing tone and timbre) with the political and historical. It is a cliché to say that poetry blends the personal and the collective, but Debeljak's skill lay in asserting the poet's individuality by emphasising, not downplaying, what he shared with the people and the place that made him. As he said in an interview, 'I cherish and relish and celebrate the multi-layered existence that is myself. That self would not have been what it is without the Yugoslav experience.'

Though he was a professor of cultural studies at Ljubljana, a penetrating but unshowy public intellectual, an editor and translator (he translated John Ashbery into Slovenian), it is as a poet that his loss is most felt, not just in Slovenia but in the neighbouring republics of the former Yugoslavia, where his belief in a republic of letters in an age of amnesia and resentment, symbolises the best of what the one-time state had to offer. He established a journal dedicated to keeping open the lines of communication between intellectuals and thinkers of every country of ex-Yugoslavia, and he is mourned across their borders.

His most recent book to appear in English is the 2009 *Smugglers*, which came out in 2015 from BOA editions in a fine translation by the American poet Brian Henry. The book is full of precise recollections of places – the streets and scenes of Ljubljana – filtered through personal and collective memory that amount to a sort of haunting of the present, being a ghost in one's own here and now. Brian Henry is exact when he describes Debeljak as the city's 'medium' more than its 'flâneur'. 'Lightbulb', one of the last poems of Smugglers, begins:

It is not magnificent, but from where I'm standing my world is quite generous. Teachers without schools and translators from languages only fish still know have taken their usual table. In an unilluminated

lightbulb, under thin glass, two are already a crowd.

The poem ends: 'A full hand, open eyes: / we are brittle and hard like paper on the run from embers'.

Debeljak was married to the American writer Erica Johnson Debeljak, who survives him with their three children.

Laurence Lerner (1925–2016)

contributed by Gabriel Josipovici
I don't think I ever told him, but one of the reasons I applied to the newly-formed University of Sussex in the winter of 1962 was that Larry was teaching there. In those days you couldn't open a weekly like *The Listener* or *The New Statesman* without finding a poem or a review in it by Larry. He had also, I discovered, recently published a volume of poetry, *Domestic Interiors*, a novel, *The Englishman*, and a book of literary criticism, *The Truest Poetry*. If Sussex are happy to employ someone like that, I thought, then it's the place for me.

And indeed it was. Larry was only one of a galaxy of brilliant and individual minds assembled by David Daiches in those early years. Gāmini Salgādo had rejoined Larry from Queen's University, Belfast, and Stephen Medcalf arrived at the same time as I did to rejoin *his* old Merton friend, Tony Nuttall. Larry was always at the centre of any gathering, talking, arguing, endlessly quoting (he and Stephen seemed to have an uncanny ability to remember whole poems *verbatim*, and not just in English). The quip went in those days that it was no wonder the University of Sussex was able to attract the best students since it included luminaries with such names as Supple, Lively and Lerner.

Larry was born in South Africa in 1925 of a Jewish Ukrainian father and an English mother. He attended schools in Cape Town and then the University of Cape Town. On a camping trip in 1945 he met Natalie, and they both promptly won scholarships to Cambridge, where Natalie studied for a PhD and Larry (typically) for a second BA. They married in 1948, and, after a spell at the new University of the Gold Coast (now Ghana), they returned to Britain and Larry found a job at Queen's, Belfast, where Seamus Heaney and Seamus Deane were among his students. Attracted by the interdisciplinary nature of the new University of Sussex, he applied and was taken on in the University's second year, 1962. In the course of his many years at Sussex, though, he was frequently absent, taking up temporary teaching posts in France and Germany (he wanted to be able to speak and read the languages, and soon did), the USA and Canada. By 1985, disliking the increasingly antagonistic politics of the era, he joined his friend and fellow-poet Donald Davie at Vanderbilt in Nashville, Tennessee. On retiring from there in 1995 he moved to Lewes, teaching more than ever on various adult education courses, walking the Downs with his friends and taking an active role in the Quaker community.

I once asked Larry why, since he was such a fine poet, he did not devote more time to it. *If I did nothing else*, he replied, *I would probably not write poetry either*. Certainly his manifold activities did not seem to stand in the way of his poetry: eight further volumes followed *Domestic Interiors*, all full of well-crafted, highly intelligent, often funny and often moving poems. Never flashy, he was, like Edwin Morgan, the master of many forms: dramatic monologues such as the brilliant and disturbing 'The Merman' and 'Written from Ypsilanti state hospital'; 'Movement' poems such as one of his favourites, 'Strawberries'; and formal experiments (though he would never have called them that or thought of himself as an experimental poet) like the poems that make up his book *A.R.T.H.U.R.*, ostensibly written by a machine. Though in later life he liked to assert that he no longer wrote poetry, only verse, there are a few poems he sent me but never published which I cherish, such as the subtle and hilarious 'Let's Play Philosophy', which begins: 'I've often wondered if we humans can / Explain just why the universe began.' It reaches a climax with

> Perhaps
> Thinking is just the way the brain cells lapse
> When things go wrong. Nobody understands
> Why we can only walk on feet, not hands,
> Why ears can't see and eyes can't hear, or why
> The price of living is you have to die.

Sadly, and, to me inexplicably, he seemed to go out of fashion when he moved to the States. He returned to England to find the friends who had been poetry editors of magazines and publishing houses had died or retired and a new generation in place who did not know him and were not interested in what he had to offer. I wonder if he made much of an effort to get his work published. I suspect not. But I feel it's a shame and I hope very much that one of these days we may see a *Selected Poems of Laurence Lerner* on the shelves. Such a volume would only confirm what all his admirers know, that his best work is among the best in the English language in the second half of the twentieth century.

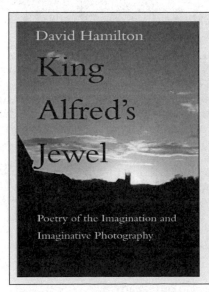

Letters

Sir,

Stella Halkyard (*PNR* 227) is, I think, slightly misinformed about Ben Jonson's thumb. Jonson was indeed arraigned and indicted at the Old Bailey in 1598 for the manslaughter of Gabriel Spencer in a duel; he was able to claim 'benefit of clergy' by reading in Latin the so-called 'neck verse', Psalm 51 – although this, as his recent biographer Ian Donaldson points out, is 'a passage that might easily be committed to memory even by the illiterate'. Donaldson continues:

His ability to read had saved him from an almost certain death. His goods however were confiscated, and, like all such offenders, he was branded with a hot iron in the fleshy part of the thumb of the right hand probably with the letter M (for manslayer) (T, for thief, mentioned in the court record, looks like a clerical error). Such a brand, immediately visible when the right hand was lifted up again in a courtroom, ensured that the benefit could be claimed only once. (Ian Donaldson, *Ben Jonson: A Life* (2011), p. 136)

So the letter must have been 'M', not 'T'. Thom Gunn seems to have deduced this in 'A Mirror for Poets', which was written while he was a Cambridge undergraduate and first published in February 1952: 'Shakespeare must keep the peace, and Jonson's thumb / Be branded (for manslaughter)…'

Neil Powell
Orford

Sir,

I read with interest the recently discovered poem by Dylan Thomas appearing in the latest issue.

There is surely a spelling mistake in the second stanza, the last word of which should be beAches, not beEches? As written it makes no sense – why would there be sand grains skating from beech trees?

Mike Jones
by email

Sir,

Mike Jones is understandably sceptical of 'beeches' (though that is the way it's spelt in the original), but he's not quite getting the image, I think. That would seem to me to be of a drowned valley, now frozen over in winter, with the drowned trees just under the surface of the ice.

The pun on beech / beach (of the lake) is therefore intentional, not a misprint, and characteristic of Thomas, who uses the drowned village, town, kingdom topos elsewhere. He's Welsh enough to resent the English flooding mid-Wales valleys for water, and fond of the legend of Seithenyn, the Welsh king who drunkenly allowed the waters of Cardigan Bay to drown his kingdom. But in any case the beaches / beeches confusion fits the dream logic of the poem: it's 'A dream of winter', not a naturalistic description of any actual landscape.

John Goodby
by email

From the Archive

Issue 28, Nov–Dec 1982
Elizabeth Jennings

LAND OF PLENTY

And there was the land of plenty.
We stood upon the edge, the frontier,
We saw the apple-blossom and the roses,
We watched the wholesome green of every vineyard.
We watched the cypresses, steadfast in winter,
Now giving shade to any who desired it.

A land of plenty-that goes back as far
As 'when my ship comes in'. We have passwords,
Keepsake language, ciphers, symbols but
Here are rich stems of tulips, here is sap
Denying gravity. We wait a cautious
Moment before we cross this frontier,
As if we trespassed on gifts undeserved.

On Reading Claudia Rankine
You Are in a Long-Distance Citizenship with You

Vahni Capildeo

The crystalline aggregation of 'microaggressions' in Claudia Rankine's *Citizen*, like a lump of geological fact, fits no human palm without spiking it somewhere. Analysis, witness, lament: the book is seamed with these modes, not composed of any one of them. It amasses its material and shifts points of view without offering settlement. In her reading at the T. S. Eliot Prize event, Rankine enjoins the audience to listen to the pronouns; to excavate the archaeology of 'I' and 'you'. Excavation would place the reader outside the poem, standing on its field of buried dreams and salient leaves of grass, spade in hand. However, such outsider privilege is disallowed by Rankine's communicative strategies within the text. The book's frequent pronoun-rich passages invite the reader to read him or herself into what is going on. What happens then?

Consider this excerpt, which was assigned for creative response in the 2015 T. S. Eliot Prize for Poetry Writing Competitions:

IN LINE AT THE DRUGSTORE . . .

In line at the drugstore it's finally your turn, and then it's not as he walks in front of you and puts his things on the counter. The cashier says, Sir, she was next. When he turns to you he is truly surprised.

Oh my God, I didn't see you.

You must be in a hurry, you offer.

No, no, no, I really didn't see you.

The first line places the reader within the anxious echo-chamber skull of someone engaged in an interior monologue, while also addressing the reader directly: a double-focus you/not you/ sometimes, almost you position is offered. This is not unusual in poetry which eschews or problematises the 'I'. What matters, in the context of the whole book, is that adverb, 'finally': the sense that this incident is one of many, that the personal is historical, that 'you' are a stone already worn down by the water-torture drips, is what Rankine seeks to convey about the predicament of the non-'white'-skinned individual whose daily life cannot be individual, cannot be pure and spontaneous – cannot be *lyric* – in so far as it is subject to the encasements and flayings of racialised perception. Rankine deals with the feeling of being heavy with time, its inescapable clay army to which the modern foot is chained, in a re-staged conversation between herself and an English writer. One point she makes, when the Englishman tries to offer her the 2011 murder of Mark Duggan in London as her subject, her black documentary duty, is that of course this could or should be his

human and writerly concern – it is his city's crime and tragedy. This is not just to do with racism being everyone's problem, or even a question of whether and when authors might reflect their locality rather than primarily racially identifying themselves across space in a kind of vatic self-essentialism. Duggan's life was annihilated in a differently understandable, time-ridden context from American murders of black youth, which drag behind them the long and intricate national-level suppressions of the inheritance of on-the-ground slavery, continuing economic inequalities, and their extra abusive inflections where gun culture reigns. The sub-title of Rankine's collection, 'An American Lyric', is one of the most revolutionary features of the book. If this is lyric, lyric must rise as a spring which acknowledges sedimentation, an inspiration which knows it breathes in shared, polluted air, which sings its body of 'you' because its 'I' is treated as an 'is not' or a 'they'.

Rankine's 'then' and 'When' slide in like acupuncturist's needles. At the first turn, 'you' has, *you* have not been assigned a gender, race or age; nor has the cashier. The microaggression, or pushiness, comes from a 'he'. The cashier exercises the power to strike the as-yet unfigured 'you' into a 'she', a female who is spoken about protectively after a mild outrage has been committed against her. 'You', you, have no option but to remain silent. The poem gives no option except witnessing silence. The poem, as an act of language, ruptures that silence, but you, 'you', languish in the drama of passivity, petrified by outrage. *Citizen*'s pronouns are not objects of excavation so much as mini-gorgons. They can turn the reader to stone. It is possible to see some agency in the verb choice 'you offer'. The cashier conferred gender on you/'you'. Now 'you'/you offers a reinterpretation of the discourtesy with which the still undescribed body has been pushed aside. When the pushing man insists that he really did not see the pushed woman, what happens? Is he apologizing? Unapologetic? Shocked by himself? This is as open as Shakespeare: the imagination can direct all sorts of tones. What does happen is that his claim stands. His claim is a disclaimer: his behaviour had, could have had, nothing to do with his own state, the excusable 'hurry' which 'she'/'you' suggests. It is that you/'you' have been (are) invisible.

Without generalizing about how distractible readers of poetry might be, or speculating about whether they sometimes wander about lost in thought rather than alert to every nuance of the notable, lived day, it is fair to say that at least some of Rankine's readers know what it is like to operate on autopilot. For reasons of fatigue, habit, disinterest in running errands, or simply not seeing what the mind does not want or expect, because of the uninflected selfishness of wanting to get through shopping quickly, rather than the special selfishness of wanting to be served first, or of not expecting a black woman (who has not imagined a black woman?) to be first or to be there at all, and therefore not seeing her. Unlike the 'you', Rankine does not offer readers any excuse for how they may have moved through her text, in an unseeing hurry or otherwise. She does not present them with characters separated out into good and bad. We have been that blind and opaque man, sometimes.

Rankine's book produced an immense personal reaction in me, and so did its reception. I have tried to separate the language of poetry and commentary from that of everyday life, otherwise what I am trying to think about would often become a thin line above a massive Derridean footnote of microaggressions: a few weeks ago, for example, my conversations with the police about a 'racially aggravated incident' at my doorstep would in the time of saying outweigh the Skype conversation about a poetry project for which I had hastened home. My reaction to *Citizen: An American Lyric* was two-fold. One, why is she holding back? Isn't everyday life much worse, criss-crossed with more violence and stupidity, than the incidents she picks? Are they meant to have the subtle portentousness of iceberg tips viewed from the deck of an old-fashioned boat? Two, where is (to borrow the title of a Kei Miller collection) 'the anger that moves'? Why my feeling of stoniness, of having stopped short, having been halted and spun about by means of pronouns? Where are the actions and reactions in return? Is it enough to register and prolong the freeze response, the bad trip, the learned helplessness? Would you offer, take, the white space around and beyond the poetry to write new, slow, powerful responses, beyond what 'you' did, or could do in the poems themselves? Finally (not to borrow, but to share, the adverb with 'you'), there is the sense of weariness at the way the book has been received, as if it is a shocking revelation, an unforeseeable testament. What have 'you' not been reading? I am truly surprised. What have they really not been reading? In the archaeology of English-language poetic heritage, what excavations have been marginalised by the cataloguers, sold off by or to the museums? For almost two generations, it has been possible to quote Kamau Brathwaite's 'Negus':

it is not
it is not
it is not enough
it is not enough to be free

Claudia Rankine continues the way that has been opened.

Letter from Wales

Sam Adams

I seem to be remarking significant anniversaries of writers and events with increasing frequency: no doubt a consequence of growing older. The year 2015 saw two that were highly significant in the annals of Wales. They are instantly recognisable to anyone with a superficial knowledge of modern Welsh history by the identifying names: 'Y Wladfa' and 'Tryweryn'.

Y Wladfa (The Colony) is the name given to the one hundred square miles of Patagonia granted to Welsh settlers by the Argentine government. We have been celebrating the 150th anniversary of the their landfall at what is now Puerto Madryn on 28th July 1865. 'A cold coming [they] had of it', the depths of the southern hemisphere winter, and a barren shore. It is even now a remote territory eight thousand miles from home, nine hundred south of Buenos Aires. They found it sparsely populated by Tehuelche hunter-gatherers who, after initial suspicion, decided to be friendly and helped to sustain them in the first terrible years. Certainly, it was nothing like the land promised in the glowing report brought back by Lewis Jones and Capt. T. Love Jones-Parry, sent out to reconnoitre and assess in 1862.

The name of Michael D. Jones (1822-98), a Congregational minister and fervent nationalist, born near Bala, north Wales, is the most prominent connected with the venture. Ordained at the Welsh church in Cincinnati in 1847, he hoped life in America, beyond the influence of England, would allow the many immigrants from Wales to hold firm to their language and customs, but soon saw this could not be. Supported by likeminded individuals and groups scattered across America, he sought other locations where a new Welsh colony might be established, and Argentina, where the government was keen to populate empty land in the south to forestall encroachment from Chile, offered the best prospect.

At public meetings up and down Wales the promise of a hundred acres each of land in the Chubut valley attracted individuals and families. Eventually, 153 (a third of them children) sailed in a small converted tea-clipper, the Mimosa, out of Liverpool, where much of the committee-work behind the venture had taken place. The hopeful emigrants included preachers, a schoolmaster, one builder, two farmers, one 'doctor', miners and quarrymen. Three-fifths were from the industrial valleys of south Wales, accustomed to heavy labour and hardship, though not of the sort they encountered in semi-desert at forty-three degrees south, between the Andes and the sea. Even if they had all been experienced farmers, it was too late to plant for next year's crops. Sheep and cattle herded overland for them were stolen en route, food and water were in short supply: it began to look like Chesapeake 1609. Some left in despair, and there were many deaths, especially among the children, but the colony survived.

Within a couple of years an irrigation project, the first in Argentina, inspired by Rachel Jenkins, a farmer's wife, began the creation of fertile wheat lands either side of the Chubut river, and the remaining immigrants were confident enough to explore farther inland and extend the colony to a fertile valley in the foothills of the Andes. Fresh waves, wavelets rather, of Welsh immigrants, five hundred or so in all, arrived within the next decade. By 1875 the new Wales that Michael D. Jones had dreamed of, where Welsh was the language of everyday life, of law and administration, education and religious observance, and every man and woman over eighteen had the vote, existed indeed. It couldn't last. The government in Buenos Aires, determined to assert its authority, insisted military conscription applied equally to the young men of Y Wladfa. In 1896 it declared that all education was to be through the medium of Spanish. Then the economic success of the colony contributed to its undoing: immigrants from Spain, Chile and Italy poured in, until Welsh became once more a minority language.

About fifty thousand Patagonians can claim Welsh ancestry; estimates of the number of Welsh-speakers in 2015 vary from 1500 to (a very optimistic) 5000. Today, there are regular cultural exchanges between Wales and Y Wladfa. Each year three language development officers from Wales spend from March to December in Patagonia promoting Welsh language learning for children and adults. The number of people pursuing Welsh courses rises year by year (985 in 2013) and a Welsh-medium primary school has been established. As in Wales, through education, a new foundation is being laid that should preserve the language for at least another generation.

~

About nine miles south of Aberystwyth on the A487, outside the village of Llanrhystyd, you see a prominent graffito, over-painted red now, on what remains of a stone wall: 'Cofiwch Dryweryn'. As he tells us in his lively autobiography, *My Shoulder to the Wheel* (Y Lolfa, 2015), Meic Stephens originally daubed it in white in 1962/3, when he and a friend 'went out into the night to paint [Nationalist] slogans on public buildings'. He was then a young schoolteacher and it was a risky business, not least because of the interest the police and MI5 took in what was construed as anti-establishment activity of any kind. This simple dictum, 'Cofiwch Dryweryn' (Remember Tryweryn) has achieved iconic status surpassing any effort by Banksy. It has become part of our national consciousness.

In 1957, an Act of Parliament gave Liverpool Corporation the right to dam the River Tryweryn in north Wales, and so drown the village of Capel Celyn and surrounding farms and farmland. The area was entirely Welsh-speaking. All but one of the thirty-six Welsh MPs voted against the Bill, but it made no difference. Immediate and widespread public protest was similarly ignored. People of Capel Celyn, men, women and children, parading through Liverpool to attend a meeting of the corporation, were vilified and spat upon. From 1960 to 1965, during the construction of the dam, protest continued and intensified. Two sabotage attacks delayed the work, though not for long, and those responsible were arrested and tried; two were imprisoned. At the official opening of the dam on 21 October 1965, a large crowd drawn from all over Wales was in no mood to celebrate. Protesters who lay in the path of the cavalcade of visiting dignitaries and escorting motorcycle police were dragged away. Alderman Sefton reached the podium to begin a planned forty-five minute ceremony. Pandemonium ensued; microphone wires were cut, stones were thrown, scuffles broke out. The event was abandoned – but the dam was there and the Welsh-speaking community erased.

Tryweryn was a late example of colonial exploitation. Wales as a country was defenceless against the expropriation of its land and resource by a single English authority. The city's argument that its need for drinking water gave it an overwhelming prerogative does not stand examination. In a recent television broadcast Lord Elystan Morgan, who as a young lawyer defended the Welsh saboteurs, said the water Liverpool took (and still takes) without payment was sold on as industrial water to twenty-four other English authorities.

The historian Wyn Thomas argues that 1965 was a turning point for Wales and that successive Welsh Language Acts and the establishment of a National Assembly have flowed from the humiliation of Tryweryn. But the language is still under threat, not least because a minority of the population here have no love for it and, with a few honourable exceptions (J.R.R. Tolkien comes at once to mind), no-one in England cares a jot. If this is still a United Kingdom, as is alleged, politicians, television, radio and newspapers should play their part in educating the British public at large about the Welsh language, and inspire all with the desire to preserve it. As things stand, the disdainful indifference of Westminster governments and the metropolitan media to the fate of one of the precious ornaments of European culture, with a literature older than English, remains persistent and damnable.

To 'write as I paint my pictures'
Paul Gauguin as Artist-Writer
Linda Goddard

'When Paul Cézanne wants to speak [...] he says with his picture what words could only falsify.' In *The Voices of Silence* (1951), French author and statesman André Malraux expressed his view that the Post-Impressionist painter could only 'speak' with paint, not with words (his letters, according to Malraux, amounted to no more than a catalogue of petty-bourgeois concerns). This gives a fair idea of the reaction that a painter who tried their hand at writing could expect in the nineteenth and early twentieth centuries. But what did this mean for artists who wished to respond, verbally, to their critics, or for whom writing and painting were equal components of an interdisciplinary practice?

I have been investigating Paul Gauguin's (1848–1903) solution to this problem. Although skeptical of critics (he claimed that art needed no verbal commentary), the French Symbolist painter – best known for his vibrant paintings of Tahiti – nonetheless wrote a good deal. His literary output included art criticism, satirical journalism, travel writing, and theoretical treatises, most of it unpublished in his own lifetime. He was adamant, however, that none of this writing amounted to 'art theory' as practiced by literary critics. Instead, his aim was to 'write as I paint my pictures' – that is (he would have us believe) spontaneously, without regard to academic convention, and in a manner suited to the 'savage' he hoped to become as a result of his relocation to French Polynesia in the 1890s. Conscious of the contradiction inherent in using words to defend the visual, he insisted: 'I am going to try to talk about painting, not as a man of letters, but as a painter'.

A hybrid figure, at odds with the colonial government yet necessarily an outsider to the indigenous community in Tahiti, Gauguin used his status as an artist (that is, as we have seen, one who is typically denied access to linguistic expression) to enhance his 'primitive' credentials. For instance, he described his manuscript *Diverses choses* (*Various Things*, 1896–8) as consisting of 'childish things': 'Scattered notes, without sequence like dreams, like life made up of fragments: and because others collaborate in it'. These qualities of fragmentation, collaboration, and childlike spontaneity can be seen in one of several double-page spreads of collaged images and text, which appear artless (like a scrapbook) but are in fact very carefully put together to project a particular self-image [below].

In an imaginary 'letter to the editor' (signed Paul Gauguin, at bottom right), he attacked art critics who seek to categorise and label artistic styles and movements. Yet on the same page he pasted several newspaper cuttings (which include a review of his work, and photographs of himself and his artistic creations) – undercutting his claim that artists have no need for the support of critics.

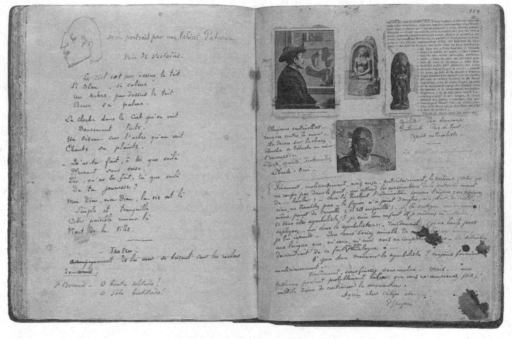

He minimised this contradiction, though, by using a careful arrangement of text and image to shift the focus away from European art criticism, and towards his affiliations with poetry and the 'primitive'. At the top of the left-hand page, he has drawn a simplified, stylised self-portrait – which he falsely attributed to 'my vahine [mistress] Pahura', as if to confirm his savage credentials. He placed it above a transcription of the Symbolist poet Paul Verlaine's confessional poem ('The sky is, above the roof, so blue, so calm') – a poem celebrating freedom and the beauty of nature, written while Verlaine was in prison for shooting his lover and fellow poet Arthur Rimbaud. The poem is followed by a reference to the twelfth-century Cistercian monk Saint Bernard of Clairvaux, quoting his praise of solitude: ('blessed solitude, only blessing'). By placing his self-portrait at the head of the page, above these borrowed texts, Gauguin links his own exile from 'civilization' to the virtuous isolation of the pious monk or the incarcerated poet.

On the right-hand page, the newspaper article at top right juxtaposes one of Gauguin's sculptures, intended to evoke Tahitian idols, with a passage from Baudelaire's prose poem 'Plans', evoking a tropical landscape, and directly compares painter and poet in terms of their rejection of materialism and experience of exotic travel. In the cluster of photographs Gauguin placed, at left, a studio portrait of himself in profile – which closely mirrors the profile of his 'savage' likeness on the opposite page – alongside his representations of Tahitian women. In this photograph he stands in front of the seated figure from his painting *Te Faaturuma (The Brooding Woman)*, whose pose reflects that of the female Buddha in the reproduction of his *Idol with a pearl* carving immediately to the right; directly below, a cropped photograph of *Vahine no te tiare (Woman with a flower)* focuses attention on the androgynous face of the woman, whose contemplative demeanour echoes Gauguin's own static pose.

Again, this visually cements his identification with the Tahitian figures. Avoiding the dull linearity of the critic, who relies on logical explanations, Gauguin's various textual and visual allusions build up a multi-faceted portrait of himself as both poet and savage – using a variety of media, authorial voices and literary registers (aphorism, criticism, poetry, polemic). This is what he meant by writing 'as a painter'.

As in his self-portraiture, in his writing, too, Gauguin experimented with adopting different identities, sometimes writing under the guise of a fictional 'ancient barbarian painter', whom he named 'Mani Vehbi Zunbul Zadi'. In *Le Sourire*, the newspaper that he wrote, printed and distributed in Tahiti, he assumed, in the opening issue, the identity of a female theatre critic (just as he drew, in 'Pahura's' self-portrait sketch from *Diverses choses*, as if through the eyes of a young girl). In a review of a one-act play by a Tahitian woman, he wrote: 'I must confess that I am a woman, and that I am always prepared to applaud one who is more daring than I in fighting for equivalent moral freedoms to men.' In the voice of the female reviewer, he goes on to describe how Anna, the play's protagonist, believes in friendship and sexual freedom, but mocks romantic love and marriage.

In a contradictory blend of sexism and feminism, combined with self-interest, that is typical of Gauguin, the review ends with a call to arms, entreating men to help liberate women, body and soul, from the enslavement and prostitution of marriage, since 'We women don't have the strength to free ourselves'. It is signed 'Paretenia' – Tahitian for Virgin. At the base of the page, next to the byline Paretenia, is a sketch of a puppet theatre, and, alongside, one of customers rushing to buy Gauguin's newspaper, with the caption 'Hurry, hurry, let's go and find *Le Sourire*'. Via the guignol, an emblem for his own satirical broadsheet, Gauguin affiliates his publication with the subversive morality of the (probably fictional) Polynesian theatre.

Gauguin aligned the visual artist with the 'primitive' and the writer with the 'civilised' but was ambivalently suspended between the two. He lamented the impact of European 'civilization' on Polynesian society, yet remained implicated in the imperialist culture that he denounced. What I am arguing is that, similarly, he wanted to assert his autonomy as a visual artist (his freedom from literary critics, 'corrupt judges' tarred with the same brush as colonial officials) but, paradoxically, he could only do so by adopting the privileged voice of the writer. His position on the margins of colonial power and local resistance – a position whose instability itself complicates those binaries – helps us to understand the situation of many others who, throughout history, have inhabited the as-yet under-studied role of the artist-writer.

Einstein and (Coincidentally) the Modern Poets

Robert Griffiths

Just over a hundred years ago, in November 1915, Albert Einstein published the second part of his relativity theory, the so-called General Theory, ten years after what then become known as the Special Theory. The first decades of the twentieth century were remarkable in physics for this theory and for ideas that were to ultimately take shape as Quantum Mechanics, to which Einstein also made early contributions. Indeed, when he received the Nobel Prize in 1921, after a decade of unrewarded annual nominations, it was for this work, not relativity theory, which was still deemed to lack sufficient empirical verification, despite Arthur Eddington's widely publicised confirmation in 1919 of the theory's prediction that light would bend in the gravitational field of the sun. Of course, Einstein's body of ideas is today regarded as the most significant contribution to physics since Newton and, for some of his admirers, perhaps the most significant intellectual event of the twentieth century; Nigel Calder is typical: 'if you have not felt the ground move under your feet while contemplating his ideas, you have missed the frisson of the century' (Nigel Calder, *Einstein's Universe*, Penguin (2005), p.6).

The first two decades of the twentieth century were also remarkable, but nevertheless in a way that seems curiously coincidental, for the emergence of what came to be seen as 'modernist' poetry in English. In exactly the same year that Einstein published his work on General Relativity, T. S. Eliot published *The Love Song of J Alfred Prufrock*, whose opening image of the evening as 'a patient, etherised upon a table' John Berryman, perhaps apocryphally, marked down as the dawn of modern English verse. In the same year, Pound made a start on his 'modern epic', *The Cantos*. 1915 was also the high tidemark of the 'Imagist' movement in 'modern' verse, through which firstly T. E. Hulme, who happened to be a mathematician and poet, and then Pound, promulgated many of the influential ideas about the apparent faults of contemporary poetry. The Imagist publications featured work by many of the other new writers: Hilda Doolittle (H.D.), Wyndham Lewis, Marianne Moore, William Carlos Williams and James Joyce, pressing an agenda based on the rejection of what was seen as the outworn 'poeticism' of their immediate predecessors. 'Direct treatment of the thing' was proposed, and the elimination of unnecessary words. There was, to some extent, a hint of the 'scientific' here, although the ostensible concern was a mere reappraisal of poetic technique.

Through the collaboration of Pound and Lewis, who was both a poet and a painter, new ideas in modernist poetry linked with the radical ideas emerging in visual art. Picasso had painted the extraordinary, multi-perspectival *Les Demoiselles d'Avignon* in 1906, the year after the publication of Einstein's work on special relativity. The Futurist movement emerged in 1909 with, as it sounds, a palpable 'modernist' agenda. Leading up to 1915, and as Europe collapsed into brutal war, Pound and Lewis worked together in the 'Vorticist' movement, which included the young French sculptor, Henri Gaudier-Brzeska, who was killed in action in 1915. For most of the modernist writers, and not merely the small group who were later to become known as the 'war' poets, the war only deepened a pre-existing sense of social decline (Pound called his civilisation 'an old bitch gone in the teeth') and the need for a new kind of art to break with the past.

It would be, perhaps the word is 'nice', to see some close links between the apparently revolutionary character of early-twentieth-century physics and the apparently revolutionary nature of early-twentieth-century poetry in English. An innocent onlooker, for instance, might wonder if a revolution in verse deemed *modernist* shouldn't be alert to the most contemporary of scientific ideas, particularly if they have an equally revolutionary character. After all, by 1915, Einstein's remarkable ideas on 'special' relativity had been around for ten years. In 1932, the critic F. R. Leavis picked out as one of Eliot's virtues that, being a great poet and a revolutionary, he had to be 'fully alive in his own time'. One might imagine that being fully alive in one's own time meant at least that one would be open to all important cultural developments, such as the scientific transformation of the human vision of the universe. Equally, if one is Nigel Calder, one might expect the earth to have moved under Eliot's feet if and when he had felt the frisson of Einstein's ideas.

However, even in 1915 Einstein and his ideas remained largely unknown to all but a few specialists. No popular treatment of even his 1905 theory was available, Einstein himself having declined to produce one on the grounds that the theory would be incomprehensible to outsiders. When it was proposed to Eddington by a Cambridge colleague that they were two of the only three people in England that understood Einstein's theories, Eddington is supposed to have paused and wondered who the third might be. It would not have been entirely fair to expect it to be Pound or Eliot, or even the mathematician Hulme or the polymath Lewis. After all, Einstein's earlier ideas on special relativity remained quite controversial, with some physicists unable or unwilling to see what they added to some previous ideas of Lorentz. Lorentz himself pointed out for instance that there was no *experimental* difference between Einstein's views and his own and claimed in 1913 that he actually preferred his own presentation of the matter (Albrecht Folsing, *Albert Einstein*, Penguin (1998), p. 216).

Einstein suddenly became an international celebrity, however, in 1919, following Eddington's famous experiment. The international media became captivated, in the long shadow that marked the end of an appalling war, with the relatively (sic) uplifting story of a still largely unknown German's new theory of the whole universe, happily confirmed by an Englishman, albeit leading to the apparent overthrow of a revered Englishman, Sir Isaac Newton. Einstein was everywhere, travelling to the USA in glory and was even invited to 'perform' in some way at the London Palladium. This 'frisson' was, it must be noted, marked by some very serious poetic work at the time. From this year dates the impeccable limerick by Arthur Buller about a young lady named Bright, who travelled much faster than light, who set off one day in a relative way to arrive on the previous night.

Nevertheless, the emerging 'modernist' poetry was not exactly *shaken* by all this populist fuss. Significantly, Eliot's landmark poem of 1921, *The Waste Land*, emerged from the mind of someone colossally educated in literature and Idealist philosophy, but with no especial interest in science and possibly even a slight disdain for it. He certainly had a disdain for the positivist methodology employed by Einstein, which, among other things, reduced the grand Idealist concepts of space and time to the operationalist banality of ticking clocks. Pound's intellectual hinterland was more varied than Eliot's, and included scientific interests, but by 1920 he was publishing the disillusioned *Hugh Selwyn Mauberley*, a typically modernist glitter of multiple voices, similar to *The Waste Land*, yet with a remote bitterness out of tune with anything that might be inspiring popular fervour: 'a tawdry cheapness / Shall outlast our days'. Furthermore, the sorts of pressures towards the modernism we find in Eliot and Pound and other 'moderns' gives us at least some clues to what seems a fairly muted reaction to revolutionary contemporary science among the revolutionary new poets.

None of the important new poets and writers in English, even if they took an interest in scientific subjects, were really in a position to respond to the forbidding technicalities of the new physics, and therefore to its precise implications for the nature of the universe and our experience of it. Contemporary artists were going to farm from Relativity Theory broad, largely 'philosophical' views about the relational nature of space and time and the loss of an absolute reality. Yet such ideas, at the level at which they were being absorbed, were ones which, for other reasons, many of the modern poets were already prepared, so that they may not necessarily have regarded them as particularly revolutionary. Einstein was teaching the relativity of time measurement, the loss of absolute time. Yet Eliot, from his philosophical studies, would have been well aware of McTaggart's attempt in 1908 to show the 'unreality' of time, which may have unconsciously inured Eliot to talk of its mere relativity. Other modern writers, such as Hulme and Lewis, were under the influence of the philosopher Henri Bergson. Bergson presented a complex theory of time-perception which emphasised subjectivity and rejected the conceptualisation of time in terms of spatial categories, a tendency he observed in both common-sense and physics. Hulme was coming under Bergson's spell by 1909 and Bergson's scepticism about the scientific treatment of time would not have encouraged Hulme to sympathetic towards Einstein's ideas.

Equally, radical views about the nature of space and about the dependence of space on the subjective point of view were among the dominant philosophical ideas that were already emerging from the early-twentieth-century revolution in the *visual* arts. Picasso's work presented figures from multiple simultaneous viewpoints. However, the direct influences on Picasso were not specifically scientific, and relativistic ideas did not occur early enough to affect a ground-breaking work like *Les Demoiselles.* Picasso's main influences were artistic, notably Cezanne and then, critically, African sculpture. Many of the modernist poets were also influenced less by contemporary scientific developments than by sources far-flung in space and time. Eliot admitted that his early poetry was most affected by Elizabethan drama and the late-nineteenth-century French poet LaForgue. The sought-for stripped-down modernist 'hardness' of Imagism that Pound saw, for example, in H.D., he viewed essentially as the collision of classical Greek against the flabby poeticism of late-nineteenth-century verse; 'It's straight talk,' he said, 'straight as the Greek'. Pound's own later verse was also heavily influenced by foreign culture, in his case exposure to classical Chinese and Japanese art. Alec Marsh has suggested that it is actually Pound's exposure to these influences that 'permanently altered the direction of literature in English' (Alec Marsh, *Ezra Pound,* Reaktion (2011)).

So even if the modernist poets had been aware of Einstein's ideas, as they presumably were at some level at least after 1919, the mathematical technicalities of professional physics and the lack of any popular treatments of this work, meant their awareness would have been at a fairly general, philosophical level. But the general ideas of spatial and temporal measurement as relative may not have been ideas that seemed surprising given philosophical and artistic influences to which they were already exposed. It was not their complete obliviousness to Einstein that may explain the limited influence of his ideas over their work, but more the way in which the general consequences of his outlook were consistent with ideas which they may have already been considering for other reasons.

Throughout the 1920s and later, members of the 'second generation' of modernist writers did respond more explicitly to Einstein. William Carlos Williams wrote a eulogistic poem 'St Francis Einstein of the Daffodils' in 1921, to mark the scientist's visit to the USA. In 1929, Archibald MacLeish also published a long, philosophical poem about the scientist. Most strikingly, although it was many years later, after the Second World War, Williams – no doubt increasingly concerned about Eliot's version of modernism, as opposed to his own – went on to argue that the whole structure of what by then he called 'modern' poetry should somehow explicitly reflect Einstein's discoveries, and he tried to incorporate relativity theory, rather obscurely, into his theories of poetic 'measure', somehow putting the scientist's theories at the very heart of his own conception of poetic form. He made this famous clarion call in 1948:

How can we accept Einstein's theory of relativity, affecting our very conception of the heavens about us of which poets write so much, without incorporating its essential fact—the relativity of measurements—into our own category of activity: the poem. Do we think we stand outside the universe? Or that the Church of England does? Relativity applies to everything, like love, if it applies to anything in the world.

One imagines, though, that the Church of England did feel it stood, to a large extent, outside the universe. Perhaps T. S. Eliot felt much the same as by then he had been long lamenting the 'weariness of men who turn from God [...] Dividing the stars into common and preferred'. Also, Williams's proposal was necessarily rather general and related only tenuously to the hard detail of Einstein's ideas. Alan Friedman and Carol Donley try to persuade us of some much richer relationship between Williams's actual poetry and the conceptual implications of Einstein. They want, for instance, to talk of the appearance in *Paterson* of 'multiple viewpoints and relativistic space-times' (Alan J. Friedman and Carol C. Donley, *Einstein as Myth and Muse*, Cambridge (1985), p. 71).

The problem here is it is unlikely that these concepts can be given in poetry anything but a fairly general, philosophical substance, unclearly related to specific scientific concerns. For example, highly disjointed multiple viewpoints were a feature of both Eliot and Pound's verse and their use is not radically more distinctive in Williams. Nor is it clear how their use *specifically* reflects a position of

Einstein's. On the other hand, it is not at all clear what manifests, or could manifest, the appearance of *relativistic* space-times in Williams's verse. It is not even clear that such a conception is coherent.

For all this later initiative of Williams's, a sense of 'modern' poetry emerged in the first two decades of the twentieth century without any really explicit recognition that it was being written in a revolutionary new scientific age. Einstein was working away in the Patent Office, altering the course of modern physics; Eliot, Pound, Hulme, Lewis, Joyce and others were working in London and Paris on poetry and fiction that would be seen as a clear break with the past. Still, it is not clear that the fact that this conjunction of events was largely *coincidental* is something anyone should particularly lament. In a pertinent account of the parallel lives of Albert Einstein and Sigmund Freud, Richard Panek tells an enlightening story of the only time these two great scientists actually ever met (Richard Panek, *The Invisible Century: Einstein, Freud and the Search for Hidden Universes*, Harper (2009)).

Einstein recalled that he enjoyed the meeting immensely, but largely because he knew absolutely nothing of psychology and Freud knew absolutely nothing about physics. Here were the two greatest scientists of the first two decades of the twentieth century, completely oblivious to the work of one another, and one at least was very thankful for it. So it was to be expected, really, that Einstein was able to completely transform our understanding of the natural universe while simultaneously (non-relativistically speaking) a number of highly cultured, but not especially scientific, individuals were leading the transformation of modern English poetry. The fact that all of this revolutionary poetry and physics (and psychology), as well as a great deal else, was going on in a mutually unrelated way probably makes it even more interesting, a sort of acknowledgement of the (relative) randomness of the extraordinary. It would, perhaps, be 'nice' to find very much more explicit connections between these two revolutions but perhaps we make rather different things much less interesting by always looking for ways in which they are more similar.

Imprudent Remarks on Certain Prudently Unidentified Literary Giants

Frank Kuppner

0. Nothing expresses the inexpressible.

1. How surprisingly easy it is, when talking about the Incommunicable, to forget that it is, simply ... erm ... *incommunicable*. (Yes. Oh indeed, Eck. They seem to claim modestly enough that they know absolutely nothing whatsoever about the Transcendent or the Otherworldly – [by the way, is that one thing or two? (or just one infinity or two?)] – but they are forever talking as if in fact they *did* know about it. (Indeed. And rather a lot about them at that.))

2. (Yes. It seems to be particularly difficult to stay silent for long about the nature of that which cannot at all be put into words.)

3. Certainly, what exists and what gets put into words have a very imperfect overlap. But this has nothing whatsoever to do with transcendence as such. (Can one completely describe, for instance, even, say, a mere, routine *sneeze*? (Leaves falling from a single tree – of many, one? (Or do fish perhaps *transcend* the net when they escape through its meshes?)))

4. ... consists in the ingenious decking out of conceptual utter-impossibilities in such finely detailed speculative verbal finery that the sheer

impossibility becomes difficult – (in an ideal world: also impossible) – to discern.

5. Since we cannot remotely succeed in dealing with this functionally infinite but merely material world in all its vertiginous complexity, we invent symbols, in order to give the impression (if only to ourselves) that we more or less somehow or other *can* do so.

6. Yes, Art. How the real, merely physical world keeps *getting in the way of* our higher, more immaterial experiences!

7. No. That which is completely other cannot be caught, *to any extent whatsoever*, in verbal representation. (But what of that? X can't be represented – so here's a *metaphor* for it. A symbolic hint, etc. etc.) (Yes. There's no way it can be described – so here's a nice description of it anyway, sort of.)

8. Talking about the Incommunicable in the *least misleading* terms! (Obviously, insofar as one actually communicates anything, one has *ipso facto* failed [to communicate its essential nature].)

9. The overwhelming poly-plenitude of reality is at least hinted at by the fact that it can be so

thoroughly misdescribed in so numberlessly many and captivating ways. (In itself, of course, something of a back-handed tribute to the peerless imaginative resources of the human, would-be superhuman mind.)

10. There are by now some very familiar signposts on the well-trodden *via fantastica* (not to say, downright *delusiva*) towards the ultimate merely quasi-superhuman existential insights. Perhaps we can use as absolute terms words which, in the merely real world, only ever have relational application ('good', 'bad', 'above', 'kind', 'loving' etc.) Or employ phrases and metaphors the key terms of which are semantically not quite transferable, not convertible into any mere mundane realistic signification. ('Light' (*n.*), 'in unknown dimensions', 'outside of time', for instance – though I dare say these will, much as usual, be the wrong instances. (They pretty well always are.)) If necessary, add for seasoning a few of the many prestigious names who have managed to get away gloriously with this sort of thing already. (Indeed, who may have managed pretty well to make an entire multi-volume career out of precisely these transcendental *tricks*.)

11. With heroic and incessant labour he set out to build a magnificent bridge between two great realms. Then, having at last achieved his aim, he set off triumphantly across it – but, alas, fell in.

12. All our supposed bridges into *the Beyond* are in fact mere piers, Heart.

13. Any noise, or air-current, or smell, or vibration (etc.) which one cannot identify (perhaps a phenomenon so subtle that one cannot even register it consciously) may possibly indicate – (no, *scrub* that) – *almost certainly* indicates – the existence of a completely different world (why not call it, say, a 'realm of existence'?) 'beyond' or 'behind' the actual one. (Possibly 'above' it. Though probably not 'beneath' it, or 'to the side of' it.) In short: any unknown or unidentified object or phenomenon making a noise or vibrating or moving (particularly if in a darkened room) is possibly – no, no, no: is very likely – no, no: is damn near *certainly* – a message or, at the very least, an emanation from the Inconceivably Other. (Frequently a completely unintelligible message – but you can't expect everything, can you?)

14. As if the human perception of significance couldn't be tricked! – just like more or less every other piece of human mental apparatus. (Particularly where evaluatory functions are involved. This smoke-and-mirror-work is surely what so much vague but sonorous verbal resonance really amounts to – [and, a small voice not quite my own gently whispers, maybe most wordless music too?].)

15. We emerged along with the world we are trying to explain, within it, as an integral part of it. It is not some completely alien medium, into which we have as it were been 'dropped' or 'thrown' [*missed!*], with perceptual apparatus that could perhaps be utterly ill-suited to it. The question as to whether our surroundings might be alien to us is already settled in the negative by the very fact that they *are* our surroundings. (And, for that matter, that we are part of theirs.)

16. Mankind (*etcetera, etcetera*) grew up and developed over these ridiculous squifillions of unimaginably long quasi-irrelevant years within *this particular universe*. The outer and the inner worlds *must* match up rather thoroughly, since they arrived here in tandem, as conjoined parts of the same integrated system.

17. In short: the external world has itself crucially formed and shaped this complex and specific perceptual apparatus whereby we interpret it.

18. (And surely the transcendent world(s), if any, is (are) indistinguishable from nothingness?) (To us, at any rate. There is nothing more to be said about 'it'. (To say more is always delusional, one way or another.)) ('It' – in short – 'is' – in short – 'there'.) (Something like all that?)

From the Journals of R. F. Langley

The poet R. F. Langley (1938–2011) was also, privately, a prolific prose writer. Extracts from his journals, which he began in 1969, first appeared in *PN Review* in 2002, and a selected volume, *Journals*, was published by Shearsman in 2006. The notes to Carcanet's recent edition of Langley's *Complete Poems*, edited by Jeremy Noel-Tod, cite a number of unpublished journal entries that directly informed the writing of his verse. The following extract, which has been transcribed by Noel-Tod and is published with the permission of the Langley Estate, refers to the poem 'Still Life with Wineglass'.

6–8th March 2001

[On *Mercury and Herse* (c.1625) by Cornelis van Poelenburch, seen in the Royal Academy exhibition, *The Genius of Rome 1592–1623*.]

But here this is. A foot across, on wood though not copper, Mercury and Herse. Here he comes, way back and up high in the summer air, in a faint rosy haze, sunshine on parts of him, superman sprinting through the sky thrusting his caduceus ahead with his right arm. Below, the procession to the shrine of Minerva, which is in dead centre, a square tomb-like structure, half in gentle shadow, a front panel let into its front face with a bevelled edge catching a shine of light gleamingly. Front left, a priest, in white, with red-crossed braces, seated back to us, with something across his knees – a plank with a box on it – can't see – a dark cow or bull, rump to us, on his left, one of the three daughters, dark hair, blue dress, turning to him, looking down at him, the dress caught up to hold flowers. Between him and her, in a golden dress, facing right in profile... Herse, blond, and the third sister, in red, draped on her shoulder. Down the slope beyond them, moving centre to the shrine, the procession, dulled and paled by the haze, but meticulous; the procession, a man on horseback amongst them. A river down there, foaming in shallows, creamily to the right. Back left a ruined city, half in a cliff worn with caves, a broken wall standing forward into sunlight, out of a slant shadow, high ground, plateau, greensward, minuscule figures. Back right, the distance, hills, Mercury overhead, advancing.

This picture has air and light, subtle temperatures, lucid colour, precious handling. I think of the wineglass of water I have been placing in the sun on the windowsill in Dovecote bedroom in order to write a sequence of poems about it. The concentration. The tiny bright silvering of bubbles inside the glass, the images of small goldfinches on thistles, incandescent thistledown, wading birds out in full light on reflecting estuary mud, bright particulars again. Here coupled with the magic of myth and this odd story, familiar to me from the Fitzwilliam Veronese, obviously popular among these Roman associates of Bril...

It places the brightness and preciosity of these small scale artists into the air and light, wonderfully gradual, suppressed yet clear. The dark girl would be Aglauros, I guess. Firm poses. Decorous, but in the open air. You can get lungs full from this tiny area, of the spring and summer I am hoping for, with classical calm and with perpending miracles. What miracles? Mary has a copy of Cage's second book: *A Year from Monday*. A Hindu and a Zen priest come to a swollen river. The Hindu begins to cross by walking on the water. The Zen man calls him back, shocked. That is no way to cross... and he takes him round to the nearest ford. That sort of miracle.

Ingeborg Bachmann

Bohemia Lies by the Sea

(*Böhmen liegt am Meer*)

translated from the German by Frank Beck

Even if houses here are green, I'll step inside one.
If the bridges are well built, I'll walk on solid ground.
If, in every age, love's labor must be lost, I'll gladly lose it here.

If it's not me, it's another who is just as good as me.

If a word borders on me here, I'll let it border.
If Bohemia still lies by the sea, I'll believe in the sea again.
And, still believing in the sea, I can hope for land.

If it's me, then it's anyone and might as well be me.
I want nothing more for myself. I want to go under.

Under – that means the sea, where I will find Bohemia again.
Finally grounded, I wake up in peace.
From deep inside, I know I'm unabandoned.

Come, you Bohemians, sailors and dock whores and unmoored ships.
Don't all you Illyrians, Veronese and Venetians want to be
Bohemians, too? Act out the comedies that make us laugh

and those that make us cry. And err a hundred times,
as I myself have erred and never withstood the trials,
though I did withstand them, time and time again –

just as Bohemia withstood them and one fine day
won a reprieve to the seaside and now lies by the water.

I still border on a word and on another land;
I border, like little else, on everything more and more,

a Bohemian, a vagabond who has and is held by nothing,
whose only gift was to find, from a dubious sea, my chosen land.

Myvatn (i), Hannah Devereux 2012, archival photographic print, size variable

Line, 2014, archival photographic print, size variable

Steam and Snow (i), 2014, archival photographic print, size variable

Untitled (Alaska), 2012, archival photographic print, size variable

Chapel Craggs (ii), 2015, archival photographic print, size variable

Darken (vi), 2012, archival photographic print, size variable

HANNAH DEVEREUX is a visual artist based in London. Born in Lincoln in 1988, she studied at University College Falmouth and Byam Shaw School of Art, Central St. Martins. Her work explores the possibility of abstraction in landscape.

Peter Huchel

The Jewish Cemetery at Sulzburg

*translated from the German by Nicolas Jacobs in collaboration
with Gardis Cramer von Laue & Cornelia Schroeder*

Although it is one of the oldest Jewish burial-grounds and has been mentioned in records since the mid-seventeenth century, it is difficult to imagine that the Jewish cemetery in Sulzburg will one day be awarded a star in Baedeker.

I first saw the cemetery in 1925. I was walking from Staufen to Sulzburg with my friend Hans A. Joachim, son of a Jewish doctor in Freiburg. It was a hot August day. With our jackets over our shoulders, we wandered about for a while in the shade of the vineyards and trees. We were both studying German at Freiburg, brought closer by our interest in modern literature. Joachim was not an Orthodox Jew. The world of dreams, the mystical, the supernatural were not his thing. When he talked about Russian or Polish Jews, a hint of mockery could be seen on his face. He considered himself a Spanish Jew – one of the Sephardi. Moreover, because he knew that in Berlin I belonged to a circle of Eastern Jews – the Goldberg Circle – and that I was an enthusiastic reader of Goldberg's book, *Die Wirklichkeit der Hebräer*, he would call me 'a little Sabbath-goy', and laugh heartily each time it made me angry.

Along the vine-covered slopes, the vine-growers were spraying the plants with copper-sulphate. They pumped the light blue liquid from metal canisters on their backs. Not a breath stirred. Only the dry call of a wren could be heard in the brown grass. We entered Sulzburg through a narrow city-gate. It was midday. Almost all the wooden shutters were closed. Tiny streets and alleyways branched off from the wide high street. They were lonely streets, which lay deep in the shadow of the houses. Grass and moss grew among the uneven cobblestones. There was a smell of wine. Huge arched doorways, oak tubs and gigantic wine-barrels stood in the yards and in the dark cavernous entrances to the wine-cellars.

In the front gardens grew asters and sunflowers, flaunting their heads in the midday glare. Sometimes a window stood open, revealing a chandelier hung with violet, and dead flies drying on the tulle netting. On the shady side of the house were women and dozing old men enveloped in the gathering dusk. On the brass name-plates of the houses I read Bloch, Kahn, Dukas, Levy, Weil.

Jews have lived here in Sulzburg for generations. As cattle-dealers they knew the head of cattle of every farmer in the neighbourhood; as vintners they went to the vineyards as early as summer to buy up the harvest; as bakers they fetched water from the wells to mix the dough, and collected wood and twigs to adjust the temperature of their ovens. As pedlars, satchels in place, with all sorts of bits and pieces – shoelaces, cotton thread and ribbons, herbal tea, matches and candles, mouse-traps and felt slippers – they would go from house to house through the villages, usually away for six days, to return for the Sabbath.

For generations – a thirteenth-century chronicle records them as residents – the Jews strove hard to care for their children and their children's children, protecting them financially against all unforeseen emergencies. The terrible persecutions to which they were subjected at the time of the Crusades, and the suspicion that they poisoned the wells during the time of the Plague, decimated the Jews. Their communities were destroyed in the Middle Ages. Later they were able to struggle for their livelihoods as money-lenders, as the Christian ban on interest still existed. In addition, the so-called 'Jew Tax' they had to pay as 'Protected Jews' provided a welcome contribution to the empty coffers of the lords, earthly and spiritual.

When I entered the Jewish Cemetery with Joachim, the dark trees on the slope above stood out clearly against the sunlit sky. For a while we lingered in the cool of the covered funeral-hall. Then we set out up the slope, up a narrow path with stone steps, on either side of which gravestones were arranged as in a terrace. Some gravestones seemed to bend over, as if under the burden of the centuries. It was a burial ground strangely attractive in its extreme neglect. Others gravestones stood like old boundary stones, as if demarcating heaven from hell, standing there for centuries and centuries, knowing every light effect, every nocturnal noise, all birdsong, all leaf-fall, and the sound and the seeping of water.

It was possible to move between the gravestones without leaving any trace. The leaf-mould had settled layer on layer, but it still seemed to me that I was moving over an abyss of shadows – somewhere time did not exist, obliterated by the silence of death.

Five rabbis are buried in the Sulzburger Cemetery. The symbols of their office are carved into their gravestones, above their names. The high priests' hands are shown blessing, in typical position – the palms of the hands facing each other, thumbs touching, fingers extended. However, some stones are engraved with a hand carrying a ewer, the coat-of-arms of the Levites, who assisted the rabbi with the washing of hands. Many gravestones are crowned with a rosette. On children's graves – half the height of the others – a small rose in half-profile is to be seen. All these old gravestone are covered in brown moss and overgrown with lichen.

About half a year later I revisited the cemetery, this time on my own. Beyond the fence, I went up the path covered in pine-needles. Torn spider-webs stuck to my forehead. It was evening. Gradually darkness took possession of the place. It began to rain and I sought shelter under a tree. I was overcome by a smell of rotten leaves and damp moss. The rain spattered the stones, penetrated the roots and the earth itself. A mist hung between the gravestones.

I saw the Sulzburger Cemetery again in 1973, after almost fifty years. I had already begun to feel discomfort on the last lap of the journey. Through the trees – the ashes, alders and willows – which grow along the narrow banks of the stream of the Sulz, I saw an encampment of cars and caravans. It was a shocking sight. When I crossed the little wooden bridge to the cemetery, I was in the middle of a camp-site. Everywhere notices in at least three languages told me what I should and should not do. But nowhere was there a sign to the Jewish Cemetery. I looked for its gate between unfolded sun-shelters and deckchairs. Laughter and fragments of conversation surrounded me. A young man and a girl, holding each other close, lay under the row of pine-trees, which separated the campsite from the cemetery – as if love could find no other place. No fine madness of the kind one reads about in old French novellas emanated from this pair – no communion of lovers at the edge of the grave, no apotheosis of death and procreation. They were surrounded by the tawdry objects of everyday luxury – plastic cups, inflatable mattresses, and Coca-Cola bottles. Like all the others, they were there solely to rub each other with nut-oil and enjoy the holiday.

There was an atmosphere of informality that did not please me. A young woman asked me, 'Do you want to go to the Jewish Cemetery?' and showed me how, by lifting the metal latch, I could open the iron gate. I looked at the caravans, to my right and left, at their monotonous white surfaces, which reflected the hard light and surrounded the cemetery from three sides. Was I witness to yet another battle between unequal opponents? Between keep-fit badminton-playing day-trippers with sweaty faces and the dead Jews who lay here in the cemetery. Nothing seemed to have changed. Certainly I was unfair on those holiday-makers, but at that moment their faces seemed so smooth and vacant, like the empty marble of the back of a gravestone.

What would I have given not to have been here! But now I was here, I forced myself through the iron gate and entered the ghetto of the dead.

This cemetery, surrounded by caravan culture, now seemed archaic, where the absoluteness of death reigned. Haste, worry, hope – all were decayed. For the dead, decline and fall did not exist. The sandstone graves patiently bore sun, wind and snow. They had been brought here by cart from the nearest quarry, then carved and then set up to commemorate the dead. The carefully chiselled Hebrew letters were eroded by the rain and on many stones were illegible.

Beneath the terracing, to the left, relatives of Jews who used to live in Sulzburg have put up a memorial. I read: 'Dedicated to the victims of the persecution of the Jews from 1933 to 1945, and in memory of the abandoned Jews of Sulzburg and Staufen who, without protection, suffered death for their belief. Erected on the thirtieth anniversary of the extermination of a venerable and devout community – 1970.'

No one was there with whom I could have spoken. My eyes hurt from the bright milky light as I read the names of the victims – Bloch, Kahn, Dukas, Levy, Weil . . .

At that moment, I missed my friend Hans A. Joachim, but he had been arrested by the Gestapo in 1942 in Nice and since recorded missing. Slowly I reached the main road lined with lime trees. My gaze returned to the gravestones, which stood between luxurious growths of bracken, faded knotweed, mare's-tail and buttercups.

Meanwhile I thought I detected voices, a light brushing of the wind in the emptiness. Under the branches of a hazelnut tree, I found a row of gravestones almost totally sunk into the earth. A few steps away, the roots of a fallen birch-tree had lifted a gravestone completely out of the ground.

On the right of the main path, in three layered terraces, stood the gravestones of the previous century and the beginning – till the thirties – of this one. Almost all have Hebrew or German lettering. There design is often in turn-of-the-century style, with much marble, pillars, and even obelisks. In fact, they differ little from the Christian funeral monuments of the same period.

Late in the afternoon I returned to Sulzburg to see what was left of the synagogue. The outer walls of the building are still standing on a slight elevation between two narrow streets. What remains is the portico, consisting of two pillars. Nothing can conceal the horror of the destruction – the wide-open hollow eyes of the windows, nailed up with planks, the ruined interior, the fallen beams, the rubble. The new work begun on the windows was an insult to the eye.

Staring in the dusk into the empty space of what was the synagogue reminded me of the ruins of the Warsaw Ghetto, of the remains of walls scorched by fire, stumps of chimneys, and iron girders rearing up like skeletons.

At the beginning of the fifties, I drove from Cracow to Warsaw by car. It was summer and the white threads of spiders' webs drifted over the stubble. No Jews were to be seen in the once so richly Galician Jewish villages. In Warsaw I visited the Jewish Museum and saw the two great milk-churns in which, shortly before the total annihilation of the Ghetto, the Jewish Community hid its most important documents, burying them with the churns – an archive of suffering which fire and destruction could not touch, a legacy in search of its heirs.

No one among the Jews of Sulzburg before the 9th and 10th of November 1938 would have thought that one could destroy a synagogue and desecrate gravestones without an investigation, indictment, or legal process. Sulzburg was their birthplace where, at their mothers' skirts or a children's maid's, they learnt to take their first steps. Here they went to school. Here they breathed their first scent of a rose or of lilac, and walked across the market-square, with greetings here and there. People were friendly. No other home existed except for this piece of earth, which they never wanted to relinquish. Christians and Jews, they all had their daily worries – the vines and their maladies, tree-felling, the harvest, cattle disease, mortgages, interest.

Now everything was different. Some Sulzburger Jews left the country. Scurrying from pillar to post, hours waiting in vain in government offices, endless chicanery till they acquired the necessary documents, the official signed permission to emigrate. Others hesitated. They were First World War veterans and felt as German as one possibly could. They would not give way to a mob of criminals and highwaymen who had simply ganged up and put themselves in uniform. They simply could not imagine that their fellow citizens would approve such a crime, and continued to hope that this apparition would pass.

The swallows with their long pointed wings swooped round St Cyriac's Church. The Jews wore their yellow star, the Star of David. There followed days and nights when the abyss grew nearer. Apprehension grew, gloom descended, wind and rain came. Rust-encrusted iron was found in the stream, and the body of a dog. Rumours abounded. For a long time, the Jews lived like people awaiting the completion of a punishment, not knowing what crime they had committed and why they should do penance. 'There is a people robbed and spoiled; they are all of them snared in holes, and they are hid in prison houses: they are for a prey, and none delivereth; for spoil, and none saith, Restore.' *Isaiah* 42/22.

On 22 October 1940, in the morning at about nine o'clock, the local gendarmerie came with a bus and took away the last Sulzburger Jews, some twenty to thirty-five people. Each was allowed to take what they could carry, plus a hundred marks in cash and food for four days. The Sulzburger Jews were deported with the Jews of Baden and the Pfalz to Gurs in Southern France. With the execution of Samuel Kahn-Rieser and Leo Louis Kahn-Baendel in Auschwitz in 1942, the four-hundred-year-old Jewish Community of Sulzburg ceased to exist.

~

Two Poems
Judith Willson

Keys, lightly touched

Three pieces from György Kurtág's piano work 'Games'

~

Flowers We Are, Mere Flowers...
(...embracing sounds)

at the bridge we joined hands

we walked until they [...]

we were not permitted to cross

and at the bridge they [...]

and at the bridge we [...]

at the bridge we joined hands
we lay in the meadow grass

Perpetuum mobile (objet trouvé)

when yellow leaves blow round the statues
    where girls in a playground run singing
        green branch green branch the gold gate is open

when vines are set fire on a hillside
    where night gathers under a river
        when yellow leaves blow round the statues

when bells spill silver over dark water
    where the chess players' tables are empty
        green branch green branch the gold gate is open

when girls' plaited hair is a skein of smoke
    where their swinging arms are a falling arch
        when yellow leaves blow round the statues

when a river is a song that swims under ice
    when yellow leaves blow
        when the gold gate is open

≈

Scraps of a colinda melody – faintly recollected

the lamp is lit   come home
come home my nine sons

our mother calls   her voice
sharp as a star   O my fine boys

our father calls   a church bell
across the clearing   my mother

my father   we cannot step back
through the door of your ribs

we dip our rough heads to pools
smell shadows   hear light

sink under moss   winter blows
through the long bones of our legs

we slip out of your song   run
in the cadence of birch woods

[Kurtág's *Játékok* (*Games*) is a collection of short pieces that the Hungarian composer began in 1973. Originally conceived as a set of simple compositions for children learning the piano, it has grown to become an exploration of musical spaces and silences. The three titles are Kurtág's own.]

Extracts from three humorous stories
in which citizens laugh at the small troubles of their lives

Based on text from *The 'Crocodile' Album of Soviet Humour* (Pilot Press, 1943)

But Yakov had hidden his identity card in his boot!
Out of the crowd came a man with hands like spades.
For ten minutes he dragged Yakov round the floor
and the crowd was silent, watching.
Yakov closed his eyes. *Comrades* he cried.
The man pulled him up then flung him down again.
Get a piece of wood to keep him still he shouted.

*

They always sat together at an empty table in the canteen.
They corresponded by means of short notes.
I want to be in the country with you, eating cherries.
A poet once wrote that love comes when you fall
and someone falls down with you.
Kolya slipped and fell, dragging someone down with him!
The streets that day were full of April sunshine.

*

Before the Revolution I lived with my aunt
who owned a bicycle workshop near the station. *Chekhov*
she used to say, *is out of date now.* When I returned
I bought her violets and an electric kettle with a yellow flex.
She said *Don't let the Committee find out!*
I have to tell her I have been transferred to Kalinin District.
The fast train doesn't stop there.

Two Poems
Eva Grubin

Unfinished

My husband has trouble finishing things.
When he washes the dishes

he leaves at least one pot in the sink and a few pieces of silverware.
He says that my writing about this

may constitute *lashon hara*, speaking negatively about others.
'Not finishing things is *zecher l'churban*,' he adds,

a way of remembering the destruction of the Temple
which stood in Jerusalem nearly two-thousand years ago.

Now he's in the other room making the bed, which will look lovely
except for a few untucked corners, a pillow askew,

strange for a man who is slightly OCD, who can't bear
a slanted piece of paper on my desk.

                        Yesterday, he almost
finished his article on Ælfric's use of Latin in Old English prose,

and he began one of the tasks on his list of things to do.
Who needs finality when unfinishing creates a longing

for what has not yet happened?

A Definition

The Torah was given
over a span of forty years.

The words we have today, even
the marks appearing over letters, are the same
as when first made.

We find the oral law
in blank spaces between words.
The sages argued in those spaces and we learn
from their disputes.

We try to practise the laws we were given
and we give back.

We pray, grateful or angry, longing
for things, wanting
what we want: a parking space, a job, true
love, a child,
attempting to bond with what we can't know.

Declining National Culture
The Dislocated Poetics of *A Various Art*
David Herd

1. The General Category

In 1987, the year Margaret Thatcher (to whom I will return) won her third term of office, the poets Andrew Crozier and Tim Longville published an anthology with Carcanet Press. Entitled *A Various Art*, the anthology gathered seventeen poets whose work had been associated, for upwards of twenty-five years, with a network of little magazines and small presses. Two of the poets, Roy Fisher and J.H. Prynne, had received some critical attention already; the majority, including (at that time) Douglas Oliver and Iain Sinclair, were little known outside the publishing circuits they had helped to develop and sustain. As a presentation of a group of writers the anthology was notable for a number of reasons: for the quality and aesthetic ambition of its selected works; for the fact that only one of the poets, Veronica Forrest-Thomson, was female; for the claims that, as it situated the work, the anthology's introduction both made and declined to make. Without passing over the matter of quality, or the question of gender, it is the implications of the anthology's introductory statement that I want to fix on. The introduction was written by Crozier. Here is his opening gambit:

This anthology represents our joint view of what is most interesting, valuable, and distinguished in the work of a generation of English poets now entering its maturity, but it is not an anthology of English, let alone British poetry. We did not begin with this distinction in mind; indeed, had we done so it might have appeared that there were no operative criteria by which to proceed. We knew this was not the case. Why, then, make such a distinction, as though the work of English or British poets did not belong to the general category of their national poetry?

As a presentation of work with which, by definition, some readers would have been unfamiliar, Crozier's opening paragraph is notable for what it refuses. What it refuses primarily, as would strike a new reader even before the content of the claim, is ease of expression. Crozier's rhetoric, if one can call it that, is characterised by caveat and reversal, by a series of refusals to make a straightforward assertion. This style is of a piece with Crozier's criticism, but is all the more striking in this context because the introduction to an anthology is where one expects the pitch. Crozier makes an anti-pitch: 'as though the work of English or British poets did not belong to the general category of their national poetry'.

The complications of Crozier's address relate intimately to his refusal of 'the general category' of a 'national poetry'. In refusing such a category Crozier declined a default position that had underpinned the presentation of anthologies since the Second World War. To take some nearby examples: *A Various Art* was published soon after Andrew Motion and Blake Morrison published *The Penguin Book of Contemporary British Poetry* (a title that didn't notice that one of the poets included, Seamus Heaney, was not British but Irish), and was soon followed by two anthologies, *The New British Poetry* and *The Grandchildren of Albion*, both of which presented experimental work in the guise of nation. The anthology that mattered in this context, however, was not British, or Irish, but Donald Allen's great assemblage, *The New American Poetry*, the huge importance of which to his own work Crozier was keen to acknowledge. He doesn't name *The New American Poetry* in the introduction to *A Various Art* but he does allude to it, noting that, of the various things the poets had in common, one was an interest in 'post-war American poetry, and the tradition that lay behind it – not that of Pound and Eliot but that of Pound and Williams'; 'the practice and precepts of Ezra Pound and William Carlos Williams' as Allen put it in his own 'Preface'. Compare and contrast, then, Crozier's introductory statement with Allen's opening sentence. As Allen writes: 'In the years since the war American poetry has entered upon a singularly rich period.' Or, as he proceeds to say: 'These poets [...] are our avant-garde, the true continuers of the modern movement in American poetry.'

To underscore the point, Allen's anthology could not have been more important to Crozier and the poets he and Longville represented. It is all the more interesting, therefore, given the comparable intentions of the two projects, that Crozier's introduction should decline the general category that Allen's opening statement so readily affirmed. Which is not to imply a critique on Crozier's part, but is to observe that his introduction came with a very full awareness of the implications of its mode of address. What Allen's example demonstrated was the value of the rhetoric of nation to the advancement of a postwar avant-garde. The question Crozier posed was how one might articulate advanced work without reference to that general category.

In fact there were two questions. The first, as Crozier himself set it out, was why make such a distinction, or separation, in the first place, the answer to which involves a consideration of the national poetic project of Donald Davie. The second question, and the one that takes us into the complications of Crozier's rhetoric, is how, in the absence of geo-political affiliation, does a body of poetry address itself to the reader. The enduring interest of *A Various Art* lies in the answers it starts to formulate to this second question. What the anthology looks to articulate, in other words, is a dislocated aesthetic.

2. Thomas Hardy and British Poetry

Donald Davie's significance in this context is twofold. He was the first prominent critic to engage with both Fisher and Prynne, and so, by implication, with the scene Crozier subsequently presented in *A Various Art*. As he did so, however, (in *Thomas Hardy and British Poetry*), his object was to include them in a project which, to use Crozier's terms, brought poetry and 'the frame of reference of national culture' into 'mutual alignment'. To say this straightforwardly, and notwithstanding his work as a champion of Russian and American poetry, from its origins Davie's criticism is a record of an effort to contain poetic language within the contours of country and nation.

The giveaway is invariably the metaphor. In his early discussions of diction, in *Purity of Diction in English Verse*, Davie offers an image of the kind of work he meant to advocate; writing in which 'a selection is continually being made' in which 'words are thrusting at the poem and being fended off from it.' Diction, according to Davie's account of English verse, is a 'fending off', where such 'fending' is in the interest of an idea of culture. By the time he wrote *Thomas Hardy and British Poetry*, the governing metaphor had shifted. Substituting a theory of poetic diction with a theory of poetic topography, Davie's claim was that 'Hardy has the effect of locking any poet whom he influences into [...] a world of specific places at specific times'. Whereas his sense of 'diction' constituted a 'fending off', his topography has the effect of a 'locking into'. In both metaphors what is at issue is what Davie repeatedly called curtailment. 'Are not Hardy and his successors right,' he asked, 'in severely curtailing for themselves the liberties that other poets continue to take?'

The critical costs of such a curtailment are readily established. Davie's Prynne, for instance, is twice curtailed. Focusing on *The White Stones*, Davie restricts his discussion to those poems that dwell on geology, as opposed to poems that deal in, say, questions of quality or of value. Even so, an interest in geology does not render the poetry Hardyesque, and so if Prynne's topographies evade a national claim, the language itself is imagined not to. As Davie has it, with reference to 'The Holy City': 'The structuring principle of this poetry [...] is the radical demand it makes upon English etymologies [...] to follow the logic we have to remember 'trade' as meaning traffic.'

It is not wrong to find an interest in etymology in early Prynne. It is, however, misplaced to render that preoccupation in national terms: etymology, after all, like geology, tends to exceed national frameworks; the word 'trade' for instance, has its origin in the low German word 'track'. Significant as it was, then, that Davie recognised Prynne at such an early point in the poet's career, there is nowhere in his writing where his critical lexicon seems so ill at ease. *The White Stones* is a book of shifting plates across which cultures and populations migrate, the deep mobility of the language catching the profound sense of movement and circulation that for Prynne, at this moment, constituted human history.

More significant than such local misreadings, however, are the implied politics of a commitment to Hardy. One gets a sense of that politics in Davie's conclusion, when he refers the reader to the correspondents to the local newspapers: 'For such people the present is a very hard time to live in; and the correspondence columns of any local newspaper show them protesting, crying out in pain.' In some way not spelt out, Davie wanted his critical project to answer to this correspondence, the local newspaper constituting for him the basis of a polis as it had, more substantively, for Prynne's mentor Olson. Which reference returns us to the question of poetry and place, and so back to the issue of poetic Englishness. *Thomas Hardy and British Poetry* articulated a moment of division in English poetry, one in which the adjective itself was entirely at stake and in which Olson was a critical figure. There was a reading of Olson's Gloucester that could get one back to Wessex. There was also, however, a reading that propelled one out, into a recognition that, as Prynne had it, 'the Pleistocene is our current sense'.

Arguments in poetry play out slowly. One answer to Davie's influential critical positioning of 1973 was Crozier and Longville's anthology of 1987, by which time the claim to nationhood looked different again. In an attempt to distract from the effects of deregulated economics, Margaret Thatcher's government had draped itself in the flag, a gesture that aimed to curtail the movement of people even as capital was encouraged to circulate unbound. Which is not to say that *A Various Art* was a political gesture. It is to say, however, that as arguments in poetics refract politics, so by the late 1980s the implications of a mutual alignment between poetry and nation had become acutely unappealing.

3. Crozier's Setting

In one sense there is an inaccuracy (or a liberty) involved in reading *A Various Art* as a work of the 1980s, given that it selects from bodies of poetry which date back, in some cases, to the early 1960s. One mitigation of such a reading is that, in almost all cases, the poets were represented by selections that included recent work: Prynne by *The Oval Window* as well as by *Kitchen Poems* and *The White Stones*; Oliver by *Kind* as well as by early Ferry Press productions. The larger justification for such a reading, however, relates to the manner in which the anthology makes its presentation. What matters, in other words, is the way Crozier and Longville curate their materials, how they angle them into the arguments of the moment of publication. What I want to suggest by this is that by mediating the work of their chosen poets the way they did, Crozier and Longville sought to create a new poetic space; a space distinct from the histories which they had themselves worked through.

Critically determining such a space is a difficult business, since it implies the inevitably treacherous procedure of reading generally across diverse poetics. I want to take advantage of the fact, though, that since the anthology is organised alphabetically, it is the work of Anthony Barnett that sets the tone. Consider the opening lines from the opening poem, 'The Book of Mysteries', from Barnett's collection, *Blood Flow*:

Here, in the
Book
of the what?

What foolishness.

How?

In rock and tree,
and, soundlessly,

what can I ask from you?

I told you,
I told you,

I formed you, the anger and the nothing that would hold you; I, on you, hold.

What matters from the outset is that the situation of writing itself is in question. The adverb, 'Here', takes us both into the book itself – or a least, a book – but also, through the book into a version of the landscape. Neither is presented with any certainty, hence the questions, and against the background of that uncertainty the poem wonders how it can address its interlocutor, an addressee who, in the context of the anthology, feels like the reader. The question the poem poses is how the speaker and the addressee can be thought, as the last word has it, to hold, how they can be held. And the key co-ordinate in that relationship is the way the poem figures its landscape.

Such figuring in Barnett is characterised throughout by what one might call refusals. Take the following passages from his sequence *Fear and Misadventure*:

I walk from day to day
under an immensity
that escapes me, that I do not escape.

[...]

The ferry boat comes out of the mist fast.
It is made fast to the bollard at the quay
and rocked by the wash of a liner.
The gangplank shifts
and people about to get off are held fast
in the mist.

What the poem refuses here is the presupposition of familiarity. There is a landscape in view, what Davie would have called a topography, but it is rendered in deliberately non-specific terms. Instead of description, what one gets is a kind of grammar of positioning, the self placed in situations it cannot entirely fathom. Against which uncertainty the operations of the language itself are thrown into relief, so that – in this case – assonance ('day/escape'; 'shifts/mist') becomes the principle by which the elements of the poem are joined. Or to use the term from the poem itself,

it is the poem's qualities of sound that make the poem 'fast'; the language, in its hesitant shaping, serving to establish a basis for relations.

Barnett is a most deliberate poet, highly conscious – even relative to the company of *A Various Art* – of the suppositions his poetry should and should not make. What he establishes, nonetheless, are qualities of expression that one finds repeated across the poetries of *A Various Art*, forms of utterance that have the effect of holding the landscape at bay. Having heard it in Barnett, one hears it in John Hall (in his great poem 'Couch Grass', for instance), in John James's refusals to enter the Welsh geographies it apparently invokes, in the abstractions of 'Thoughts on the Esterházy Court Uniform' and 'The Oval Window'. Various as *A Various Art* is, then, there is, nonetheless, a curatorial principle at work, the purpose of Crozier and Longville's anthology being to establish a distance between poetic utterance and the specifics of the national geographic – precisely, as they saw it, so that the poem could do its work.

A test case, in the context of such a curatorial project, is Roy Fisher, a poet easily situated – by Davie not least – as a poet of observational and situational realism. It is interesting to notice, in this connection, that Fisher's poem *City* is represented in *A Various Art* only by a single, highly reflexive prose passage. It is interesting also to consider that Fisher, or rather Davie's Fisher, was the subject of an essay Crozier wrote around this time as a commission for a festschrift to mark Davie's retirement from Vanderbilt, but which was rejected and which Crozier eventually published in *PN Review*. As it was eventually published, Crozier's essay is a finely tuned, extended critique of Davie's Fisher, the point of difference being the degree to which one could read poetry and place in relation to one another. For Crozier, the whole point was to open up the differential between them. This, as he saw it, was the purpose of Fisher's inquiry. Expressing himself as carefully as ever, Crozier contended that:

The observer's own life, the past of the city, sexuality and death, are thrown into question, conditions of existence that struggle for expression against the grain of their locale, but which obtain recognition there by Fisher's observation of their negation or occlusion in the presence of the city's corporate signs.

As Crozier reads Fisher, the locale does not enable expression but thwarts or occludes it, an interpretation that allows the question of topography to become a question of politics. As he puts it, drawing out Fisher's relation to his environment:

If Fisher looks for meanings beyond those [...] already [...] socially produced, his objectivity is nevertheless no more than heuristic. It has probably galled him to find his writing so consistently praised as description, a type of scrupulous realism.

Crozier's reading of Fisher, as resisting the seductions of the locale for the reason that the meanings of the locale are socially produced, feeds back into the terms of his introduction to

A Various Art. As he puts it there: 'poetry, if it is an art, is an art in relation to language in general; its artifice is various, and its rules apply to specific rather than general occasions'. The key word is 'art', a term by which Crozier repeatedly opposes the implications of 'culture'. He distinguishes the poetry he admires from work in which, 'the signs of art had been subsumed within a closed cultural programme'. He observes that he and Longville resisted the temptation to propose a countercultural 'Albion in place of England' because they declined 'the constructed totalities that represent national culture, however defined'.

'Culture', in this context, is one of Davie's words. Speaking of the kind of modern poet he did not advocate Davie remarked that, 'the modern artist has learnt to appreciate [styles] independent of the different cultures of which they were the flowers'. Davie makes this remark in the context of his discussion of diction, but the organic metaphor links seamlessly with this subsequent theory of poetic topography. Poetry, by this argument, to reiterate Crozier's terms, was to be in 'uncomplicated alignment' with the 'frame of reference of national culture'. Arguably there would have been a moment in Crozier's career when this would have seemed less controversial, the moment of the magazine *The English Intelligencer* perhaps, a magazine of the sixties that, in its connection to Cambridge, shared critical histories with Davie. By 1987, however, the 'frame of reference of national culture' belonged emphatically to the political right, and the task of the artist working with language was, more than ever, to resist such socially produced meanings.

4. Writing after *A Various Art*

Crozier and Longville's *A Various Art* did not have the altering effect on poetry that Allen's *New American Poetry* did. It did, however, help to open up spaces that radical thought and writing have continued to move into. Thus, the critical distinction Crozier insists on between art and culture can read like a peculiarly English affair; like an argument within a tradition overburdened by its own norms. It is a distinction Alain Badiou also makes, however, in *The Meaning of Sarkozy*, where the differential constitutes the second of eight demands he made shortly after Sarkozy's election, the first of which, Point 1, reads: 'Assume that all workers labouring here belong here [...] especially workers of foreign origin'. The connection is important. What Crozier observed in the nationalist moment of Thatcherism, just as Badiou observed in the nationalist moment of Sarkozy, is that the linguistic turn toward culture has the effect of consolidating restrictions. In both cases, in other words, the counter-insistence on art is a way of keeping the discourse of belonging open.

What that openness has enabled in terms of poetry is an ongoing rejection of the national frame, the terms of which continue to promise new formations. Tony Lopez, for example, is a poet for whom the refusals of *A Various Art* have enabled a compositional space. Take the following poem from 'Blue Shift', one of the sequences that makes up *False Memory*:

Frantic scenes were witnessed in Utopia
And important news was left out or 'twisted.'
Gazing over the visionary landscape, Joan sees
A brighter cloud from which emerges freedom:
The happy cry is taken up by the crowd –
With slimy shapes and miscreated life. It seems
A racist policeman planted the bloody rag
Giving the precise emotional push off. My eye
Turned westward, shaping in the steady clouds
Thy yellow sands and high white cliffs. O England
Ere from the zephyr-haunted brink I turn...
On the cover was a blonde with a revolver
Falling from a window. When I asked him
The boy replied: 'You just can't believe it'.

What the boy in Lopez's poem can't credit is the national frame, England, a poeticised frame within which, as here, 'A racist policeman planted the bloody rag'. What Crozier and Longville curated, in the late 1980s, was a poetic space in which a productive linguistic distancing could be achieved, in which markers of affiliation need not be inscribed as read.

Note: This essay was first presented as a paper at the National Poetry Foundation Conference on the 1980s, at the University of Maine, Orono. A version of section two, 'Thomas Hardy and British Poetry', appeared as part of 'Dislocating Country: Post-War English Poetry and the Politics of Movement', in Peter Robinson (ed.), The Oxford Handbook of Contemporary British and Irish Poetry.

Three Poems

Linda Anderson

Adagio

'Moving now toward the vicinity of hurting,
now toward the vicinity of imagining.'
(Elaine Scarry, *The Body in Pain*)

Where the lapwings had stood was now
empty and the valley sunk beneath

the light shifting of sun. You clung on
inside the notes as they swayed

between horn and oboe.
This avulsion was the body's argument.

You were somewhere between a field
and a memory. The score was still playing

as you ventured towards where the words
would fuse into you: integument, heart.

Intermezzo

You've played this before but each time
you come back to it you feel like a novice.
Your fingers won't stretch between the notes
and the chord becomes an arpeggio
the G# sounding distantly, like an afterthought.

Chords can be illuminated from within.
You've lived most of your lives and still
the soft unsounded notes summon you
to try again. In the late afternoon, you remember
her voice: *The end always comes in medias res.*

Sanctus

A history of dour prayer.
Sunday School with bullies.
A music teacher with her ruler

ready to whack fingers
for each wrong note,
each sin. Asking for

blessing from the petty-minded.
Whence cometh my salvation
this secular faith bound to

the sustained reach of a solo violin.

Two Poems
Eleanor Hooker

Thoughtless

The Arctic bear inside
her mind brought the blizzard.
He galumphs around behind
her eyes, licks saltwater
from her lens, then mists them
over with his constant panting.
He feeds on grey matter –
grinds his teeth on every little thought,
gifts her memories to snowy silence.

When she asks her husband
what'll happen when she disappears
into the frozen hush of herself,
he holds her close, says, *we won't
notice the difference*. That used to be
their joke. The Arctic bear
inside the emptying room
of her mind, sits down
with a thump.

Leave Taking

And as I wave them off,
Quiet comes to stand
beside me. She smiles too
at the inexpert weave
of the car backing up the yard.
The cheerful toot-toot on the
horn as they drive under the
arch and back to the world,
reminds me that all that occupies
the space between me
and loneliness, is quiet.

The Ephus
M G Stephens

1.

Whatever one thought personally of Joel Oppenheimer, an evening spent in his company was electrifying. You could see the man disintegrating before your eyes, and yet his voice was deep and resonant, filled with the gravel and experience of an urban blues singer, and he spoke so coherently about his passion for writing. His take on poetry was not as unorthodox as some might think. He was of the tradition, if by tradition one meant Williams and Pound, Olson and Creeley. But it was a proscribed poetics, even to the acolytes like myself. If you drifted beyond the precincts of Black Mountain, Joel could be as severe as the Franciscan monks of my childhood, whapping your knuckles (metaphorically speaking in Joel's case) with the wooden triangular ruler. Joel Oppenheimer did not fancy us writing like Frank O'Hara or Ted Berrigan, though he might complement you for writing like Paul Blackburn or Ed Dorn. He was far too vulnerable to be truly macho, and yet some of the things he said could be construed as being macho, certainly words that were not sensitive to what Frank O'Hara called 'feminine, marvelous, tough', though Joel might sanction the last type of poem – a tough one – he didn't seem at all inclined to see us write either the feminine or marvellous poem, even from the few women in our workshop class, many of whom were marvellous and tough.

2.

With five relatively short poems in the Don Allen anthology *The New American Poetry*, Joel Oppenheimer established himself as one of Black Mountain College's voices, this amalgam of Charles Olson and Robert Creeley, but particularly William Carlos Williams, who was the clearest influence upon him. Williams had been the local suburban New Jersey doctor, he was as Joel Conarroe put it, 'delivering over two thousand babies; at the same time, writing poems on prescription blanks during free moments, he somehow managed to become the most influential and original poet of the century'.[1] William Corbett, in his 'Introduction' to Oppenheimer's early poems, notes that Joel did not respond to Williams until he came upon the two versions of the locust tree poem. Corbett refers to the 'skinny plunge' of the poem, and how it became a kind of 'spine in Oppenheimer's work'. This poem is Williams at his jazzy, improvisational best. Instead of one lovely poem, there are two, almost like alternate takes on a jazz CD. The first poem, 'The Locust Tree in Flower', is eight stanzas of three lines each, only a word or two on each line. It begins:

> Among
> the leaves
> bright
>
> green

The second version is only five stanzas long, and the last stanza is only one word. Like the previous version, each stanza contains three lines of a word or two each.

> Among
> of
> green
>
> stiff

Joel Oppenheimer would write a kind of theme and variation on Williams so often in his own poetry. Here he seems to capture the spirit of these two Williams poems in one poem of his own that gets repeated three times. It is called 'Triplets':

> thus
> for
> the warm
> and loving
> heart
> the
> inmost
> and
> most
> private
> part
> shall
> ever
> be
> sweet
> eros'
> dart.[2]

As William Corbett notes, Oppenheimer's poems had the 'equivalent lean, virile and vertical rush down the pages. They move not with the passionate, impatient jolts and leaps common to Williams but with a steady propulsion' (Corbett, 'Intro', J.O.'s *Selected Early Poems*). With regard to Oppenheimer's influences, consider this Williams poem entitled 'Death the Barber':

> Of death
> the barber
> the barber
> talked to me
>
> cutting my
> life with
> sleep to trim
> my hair—

In Oppenheimer's 1962 book, *The Love Bit*, published a year before Williams died, he would – again – write his own theme and variation on a Williams poem: 'For the Barbers' is Joel's tribute to his mentor.

> tenderly as a
> barber trimming
> it off i
> sing my songs, like
> a barber stropping
> a razor, i rage.

tho the song be
pure as anything, if
the mode be not right,
if the mode

        be not pure

the calculation of
a barber is immeasurable,
the cunning, the sly
skittering about the
head
    if a needle were
dug in the middle of
the cranium would it
do more damage?

        oh the
professionals what we
should fear.

Coincidentally, there is a
Gilbert Sorrentino poem, 'Ars
Longa', from his book *Black and
White* (1964) that 'corresponds'
in its rhythms to Oppenheim-
er's own poem, and so it is a
theme and variation on another
theme and variation. It begins:

Carefully as a man tying up
    tomato plants,
they will to be arranged, the words,
they are all our concern, as that
    bright
little chainsmoker knew,

what is said is better than said if the
page be impinged upon with power.

3.

Charles Olson's influence on
Joel Oppenheimer – from Black
Mountain College outward
– was more intellectual than
stylistic. Oppenheimer, for
instance, had none of the
mythic apparatus that Olson
brought to poetry. Yet when
Olson was being tender and
lyrical, one could see the
through-line from him to
Oppenheimer. Here is Olson
writing in a poem titled 'Maxi-
mus, to Gloucester, Letter 2':

. . . . . tell you? ha! who
can tell another how
to manage the swimming?

he was right: people

don't change. They only stand more
revealed. I,
likewise
Or consider this one from
Olson's *Maximus Poems*,

entitled 'The Songs of Maxi-
mus, Song 3':

In the land of plenty, have
nothing to do with it
        take the way of
the lowest,
including
your legs, go
contrary, go

sing

4.

The contrarian singer's life
was exactly what Joel Oppen-
heimer had chosen, even after
he had become the director
of the Poetry Project, his
first responsible, established
position as a poet. Joel would
resign from his print-shop job,
a kind of work he had done
since his college days. Instead
of dirty fingernails from
printer's ink, he could get his
hands dirty writing poems. Yet
whenever Joel spoke about
Olson, it was as Joel's teacher
– Olson's classroom skills
and his marathon evenings
that stretched into the next
morning, with the master
monologizing until the sun
rose. These were stories about
Olson the man-mountain, the
six-foot-eight-inch giant of a
man; it was never about Olson
the poet but Olson the teacher.
As for the more tender, worldly
utterances, Joel saved them
to speak about Creeley, his
mentor, his model, his para-
digm. Creeley was how one
wrote poetry, whereas Olson
was how you thought about
poetry as an abstract concept,
as an intellectual idea. Olson
was aloof whereas Creeley was
Joel's lifelong friend. As far as
I know, Olson never came to a
workshop at the Poetry Project,
whereas Creeley visited several
times, doing workshops before
he gave readings at the church.
Having Creeley at a workshop
at the Old Courthouse was
a bit like having an old jazz
master show up for a class. He
even spoke the way the jazz
musicians I had known spoke,
with a lot of *yeahs* and *likes* and
other stuttering peculiarities of
speech, accentuating whatever
was being spoken about.

It was Creeley who was the
first person I ever heard say
that a poem 'works', i.e. that it
was already there, and didn't
need much discussion.

When we read Creeley poems
– I am purposefully using the
first person plural as my friends
and I would gather together
before and after workshops to
discuss and to read aloud all
these poets we talked about or
even met at Joel's workshops
– we noted how allusive some
of the simplest of these poems
were. Even a list of names
resonated for us, such as the
names in this later Creeley
poem. Joel and Gil, LeRoi,
Cubby: those names, perhaps
unfamiliar to the casual reader,
could be none other than Joel
Oppenheimer, Gilbert Sorren-
tino, LeRoi Jones, and Hubert
'Cubby' Selby, Jr – the people
who Creeley hung out with
in New York. The influence
Robert Creeley exerted upon
Joel Oppenheimer was appar-
ent in the first poem Joel ever
published, about the dancer
Katherine Litz. Oppenheimer
published 'The Dancer' in
1951 while at Black Mountain
College.

her particular
        as we too
have particulars
        but she

flies free
    pulling.

5.

Concretizing the abstract was
often a gift in Robert Creeley's
poems, whether addressing a
long cadenza of thought or a
brief perception as in his poem
'Here'.

    Here is
    where there
    is.

Joel was less successful using
pure abstraction. He was not
a philosophical poet the way
Creeley could be. Joel was a
passionate poet of the quotid-
ian, one who mined feelings
using concrete terms, almost
the way metaphysical poets of
another age expressed their

love of God or simply the spiritual realm of nature. But Joel was a student who could keep pace with his mentor on subjects that required lyrical compactness. Both Oppenheimer and Creeley had pitch-perfect ears, equally capable of rendering the spoken onto the page, making it pure poetry. No Robert Creeley poem illustrates this idea better than his legendary 'I Know a Man'. I say it is legendary because it is such a timeless poem, still fun to read today as much as it was in the 1960s, and it was certainly as iconic a poem as Frank O'Hara's 'The Day Lady Died' or Allen Ginsberg's 'Howl', at least among downtown poets, not just of my generation but also Joel's. Think of how many other literary works devolved from this short-lined sonnet. Gilbert Sorrentino derived the title of his first book of poems from it (*The Darkness Surrounds Us*); Jeremy Larner's novel was called *Drive, He Said,* also borrowed from Creeley's poem. In many respects, it is a classic dramatic monologue – a speaker, who is not identified, is filled with passion and intensity, and no doubt drunk as a skunk. It is talk, not the truth, but also not a lie, i.e., it is bullshit talk, drunken speech, meaningless, and yet somehow riveting to hear, almost the way a piece of music is. The sudden shifts, the turns in direction, feel almost like going on a drunken ride down a mountain passage or like riding a roller coaster.

6.

These were Oppenheimer's peers and mentors, going from Williams to Olson to Creeley and then to poets such as Gilbert Sorrentino, LeRoi Jones, and Paul Blackburn. The anarchist in Joel Oppenheimer also embraced a world with the kind of people that a Brooklyn poet like Walt Whitman wrote about in the Introduction to the first edition of *Leaves of Grass*:

Despise riches, give alms to every one that asks, stand up for the stupid and crazy, devote your income and labor to others, hate tyrants, argue not concerning God, have patience and indulgence toward the people, take off your hat to nothing known or unknown or to any man or number of men, go freely with powerful uneducated persons and with the young and with the mothers of families.

No longer working as a printer, Oppenheimer would have to learn to be a teacher now. Again, he probably went to Olson for help. The entire second section of Olson's 'Tyrian Businesses' (*Maximus*) concisely describes this experience of the writer in the classroom, and reads as follows:

> how to dance
> sitting down

For the next two years, Joel Oppenheimer would be the director of the Poetry Project, a sit-down job, and that is where he would dance. Those others whom Walt Whitman mentions in the Introduction to his epic poem Oppenheimer would hang out with in the Lion's Head over in the Village on Sheridan Square. They would become Joel Oppenheimer's 'stupid and crazy', and also his friends and colleagues as his drinking escalated and the pressure of running a community arts project took its toll on his mental and physical health.

7.

Oppenheimer warned us about the professionals because he was at heart a gentleman scholar and poet, an amateur in the sense that he had nothing to lose and that he did not trust the professionals to do it right. Making money from his poetry was not a criterion for greatness. The poems had an integrity all their own. But like everyone else, Joel had his contradictions, or, I should say, he was more contradictory than most. (Sometimes he was nothing but contradiction!) Baseball was one such

contradiction because the men he admired in that sport were all professionals, although being a fan of baseball, he remained an amateur, even in his enthusiasms. Unlike his sports-journalist friends at the Lion's Head, Oppenheimer was not yet paid for his opinions on sports. (That would change shortly, though.) This amateur's love of the professional sport is nowhere more evident than in his love of the knuckleball pitch, something he obsessed about in his conversations. This type of pitch is defined in *The American Heritage Dictionary*, Second College Edition, as 'a typically slow, randomly fluttering pitch thrown by gripping the ball with the knuckles of two or three fingers'. It required finesse, and as Joel notes in one of his *Village Voice* columns (8 June, 1972): 'the one thing we amurricans [*sic*] can't seem to accept is finesse, and we're always looking for the leader'. He goes on to say that this was New York, where excellence is appreciated, 'except when it smacks of conniving instead of strength'. Thus the knuckleball, about which Oppenheimer wrote: 'i know, i know – rip sewell tried to throw one (he called it the ephus, which is a lovely name for anything) past ted williams in an all star game, and williams blasted it, but williams was the greatest, and nobody else much that i recall hit it big that season.' The ephus: the knuckleball – a slow, randomly fluttering pitch – was thrown by gripping the ball with one's knuckles. Picking Joel Oppenheimer over Paul Blackburn to direct the Poetry Project was like going to the bullpen for a knuckleball pitcher. And as Joel wrote in his poem 'For Hoyt Wilhem', one of the greatest knuckleballers:

and if you keep
on doing it
eventually they let you
keep on doing it
even while they hate it
and you keep on and on

This poem about one of the

greatest knuckleball pitchers in all of baseball concludes, apropos of Joel Oppenheimer's becoming the director of the Poetry Project, though it was about baseball, too:

at least one of us guys
with nothing but knucklers
caught their attention

made them say at last
it's the right stuff
even if it does look funny

Despite the vociferous objections by some poets in the local community, Joel Oppenheimer was the right person at the right time for the right job. The poet as ephus, the knuckleballer, was the director of the St Mark's Church in the Bowery's new Poetry Project now, even if Joel called himself everyone's second choice. This was the person who was going to dazzle you with the junkball, the wizardry of knuckles on rawhide, of finesse instead of power, of letting go, of being in the moment, whether it was poetry or baseball, drinking or sitting around bullshitting. The dystopia of the East Village now had a dystopian poet as its fearless leader, and in 1966 not everyone on Second Avenue was happy about that, because not everybody followed baseball, not everyone was drinking themselves to death; not everyone was so dedicated to anarchy and mischief, to the bawdy and the irreverent, not to mention the ephemeral (the ephus!) and the irrelevant. But for a twenty-year-old would-be poet (me), it was as if this was Albion, and Joel Oppenheimer was Pan's very muse.

NOTES

1. Joel Conarroe, ed., *Six American Poets: An Anthology* (New York: Vintage Books, 1991), p. 148.

2. Joel Oppenheimer, 'Triplets', *The Love Bit* (New York: Totem Press / Corinth Books, 1962), unpaginated.

Pearl
Lines 973–1092
Simon Armitage

Note on the Translation

Heartbroken and in mourning, a man describes the terrible sorrow he feels at the loss of his beautiful and irreplaceable 'Perle'. In August, with flowers and herbs decorating the earth and perfuming the air, he visits a green garden, the scene of his bereavement. Tormented by images of death and decay, devastated by grief and overpowered by the intoxicating scent of the plants, he falls into a sudden sleep and begins to dream, embarking on an out-of-body experience that will lead to an encounter with his departed pearl, who we learn is his child, and a journey to the gates of heaven.

Probably composed in the 1390s, only one copy of *Pearl* remains in existence, surviving as the first poem in a manuscript that also includes *Sir Gawain and the Green Knight, Patience,* and *Cleanness* (or *Purity*). All four poems are in the same hand, and although the writing probably belongs to that of a scribe rather than the original author, most scholars believe they were composed by the same person, about whom we know very little.

Pearl presents a substantial challenge to any would-be translator because of its unique form and intricate structure, involving elaborate number-symbolism, alliteration, a four-beat line, rolling concatenation, and a strict *ababababbcbc* rhyme scheme impossible to render into contemporary English without falling back on archaisms or tweaking the sentence structure and subject matter beyond acceptable limits. Given those technical challenges, every decision feels like a trade-off between sound and sense, between medieval authenticity and latter-day clarity, and between the precise and the poetic. My own response as far as the rhymes are concerned has been to let them fall as naturally as possible within sentences, internally or at the end of lines, and to let half-rhymes and syllabic-rhymes play their part, and for the poem's musical orchestration to be performed by pronounced alliteration, looping repetition and the quartet of stresses within each line. So formalists and fusspots scanning for a ladder of rhyme-words down the right-hand margin of this translation will be frustrated and disappointed, though hopefully my solution will appeal to the ear and the voice.

Pearl consists of twenty sections, every section containing five twelve-line verses, with the exception of section XV which contains six verses, bringing the number of verses to an enigmatic one hundred and one and the number of lines in the poem to 1212, thus mimicking the structure of the heavenly Jerusalem: twelve by twelve furlongs in dimension, with twelve gates for the twelve tribes of Israel, as specified in the Book of Revelation.

S. A.

XVII

1

'To find a view of that flawless place
walk upstream alongside the water
to the valley head, till you come to a hill,
and I will follow on this far bank.'
Then I wouldn't delay a moment longer,
but went beneath leaves through dappled light
till I saw that city perched on its summit,
and stumbled towards that stunning sight
some distance away beyond the brook,
shining brighter than the sun's beams,
in its features, facets, size and structure
just as Saint John revealed in Revelation.

2

Yes just as the apostle John described it
I saw for myself that exalted city:
the new Jerusalem, luminously rich,
as though descended from heaven's heights.
Its buildings gleamed with pure gold,
blazing and glinting like burnished glass.
They stood on a base of precious stones
formed of twelve well-fastened tiers,
a firm and cleverly fashioned foundation,
each stratum cut from a seamless gem,
as in the writings of Revelation
where John the apostle depicts the apocalypse.

3

John had described those stones in his scriptures
so I knew their names and also their nature.
I judged the first of those jewels to be jasper,
found at the very bottom of the base,
gleaming green on the lowest layer.
Sapphire occupied the second stage,
and clear, crystalline chalcedony
shone pure and pale on the third plane.
Emerald was fourth with its glaring green finish,
and finely striated sardonyx the fifth,
and ruby the sixth, exactly as stated
by John the apostle when depicting the apocalypse.

4

John also described the chrysolite,
the stone which formed the seventh stage.
The eighth was of brilliantly white beryl,
a table of twin-toned topaz the ninth,
a course of chysoprase the tenth,
noble and elegant jacinth the eleventh,
and twelfth, most trusted in times of trouble,
was a plane of purple and indigo amethyst.
The wall above that tiered base
was jasper, glistening and glittering like glass,
a vision I knew very well from the version
in John the apostle's apocalyptic scriptures.

5

Then I saw still more of what John described:
those twelve tiers were broad and steep
with the city on top, perfectly square,
equal in every dimension, and exquisite.
The golden streets sparkled like glass,
and jasper glared as if glazed with egg-white.
Inside, those walls were studded and set
with every possible precious stone,
and every square side of that estate
in every dimension measured twelve furlongs,
in height and width and length the same size,
just as John the apostle had judged.

XVIII

1

And I saw still more of what John had scripted:
each of its aspects had three entrances,
so twelve gates in total were visible.
The portals were plated in expensive metals,
and the doors adorned with a singular pearl,
a perfect pearl that could never fade.
Over every arch in carved characters
the names of the Children of Israel were inscribed
in order of age, that is to say
beginning with the first born, and so on and so forth.
Such light illuminated the city's streets
that neither sun nor moon were needed.

2

They needed neither sun nor moon
since God Himself was their guiding light
and the Lamb their lantern. There was no doubt:

through God's brilliance the city glowed.
And all was transparent, so my gaze passed
through wall and structure without obstruction,
till I saw with my eyes the high throne
arrayed in awesome ornaments,
as John the apostle correctly recorded,
with God taking His place upon it.
And running directly out of that throne
was a river more radiant than sun and moon.

3

No sun or moon ever shone so sweetly
as the plentiful water that poured through those precincts;
it surged swiftly along every street
without sediment or slime or foaming filth.
No church or chapel had ever been built
or temple constructed within the walls;
God Almighty was their one minster,
the sacrificial Lamb their spiritual food.
The gates were never bolted or barred
but open at every possible approach,
though none may enter in search of sanctuary
who bears any blemish beneath the moon.

4

The moon cannot practice her powers in that place,
she is pockmarked and pitted and impure in person.
Added to which, it is never night-time.
How could the moon, casting her moonbeams
from celestial circuits, hope to compete
with the light that sheens off that stream's surface?
The planets are pitifully poor in comparison
and the sun too dim by some distance.
The riverbanks were bordered by bright trees
which bore on their boughs the twelve fruits of life;
twelve times a year those trees offer harvest,
their riches returning monthly like the moon.

5

No more amazement under the moon
has a human heart ever had to endure
than when I witnessed the walled city
and marvelled at its fabulous feats of form.
I stood as still as a stunned quail,
hypnotised by that holy vision,
every nerve and sense in my body numbed,
enraptured by unrivalled radiance.
And this I declare with a clear conviction:
any mortal man, having seen such a miracle,
despite the craft and cures of his doctor,
would go to his grave beneath the moon.

Blind Dates
Siriol Troup

i | The only things we believe in are the sheep and the dogs (Henry James)

Sergeant Troy, *Far from the Madding Crowd* by Thomas Hardy

He flourished his sword by way of introduction, rustling towards the hollow among the ferns.
Brass and scarlet shone, the ring of sheep-bells followed. Young and trim, by turns
serious and twinkling, he spoke of love but thought of dinner, and though I took him
for a wild scamp and a sinner, his well-shaped moustache agitated me strangely
until I grew feverish under the evolutions of his blade. He hinted - I forbade. Finally
all was over: quick as electricity, he made a hole in my heart that his tongue
could not mend. I did not flinch at his loose play or soldierly démarche. *Ah, Beauty,
bravely borne!* said he, pretending to pay though always intending to owe. Yet truth
is truth at any hour of day. The ground was harsh, the haggard night dim and starless.
Dogs barked, meek lambs bleated and panted as he fled, but still his sword strung
lanterns in the air and left me shuddering in the streams of his *aurora militaris*.

ii | Eek, ik, eeik, ik, eek

Piet Hanema, *Couples* by John Updike

High sun over the treacherous game, pink lemonade beside his chair, with strawberries, like his
mother used to make.

I serve. He crouches at the net, feeling the land around him, sniffing for lust and floods, the racket
sweating like a hammer in his fist.

Blood broods under the pale furred legs, the shadow ready to spring. Freckles bounce on his fore-
arms. He plays like a handyman, distracted by upright supports and copper plumbing, testing joints
with his knife,

something flat about him, like a greenhouse pane or an honest plaster wall. We take a break

for gin-and-Bitter-Lemon. Advantages shift. He does a handstand on the court, then slaps my
behind. Horrid slippery little man who'd eat up every woman in sight and wants the world to lick his
tool-toughened hands and find him funny when he's pissed.

He whacks the ball towards death's long canal, bragging that he's a shit, and second-rate at this, a rus-
set hamster running in his wheel. Who made the cage he's worked so hard not to inherit? Who? Who?

Lousy at love fifteen. He rejoices in the keenness of our chemistry, our symmetry, his stiffening sense
of sin. This is God's playground; he won't be mocked. There's a wife

of course, who guards his soul,

and a snug house and a solemn tugging cookie-faced daughter. He wants to fling me down on the
service line till I concede the set. He wants to sleep with me to bring his mother back to life

but he's wondering, from the height of his fear, if I'm a customer whose whims he must work with or a
dead body too rotten to screw.

I can see he's trouble, this small sad shaggy red-haired Dutch boy, watching out for seepage, plugging
every hole.

iii | When the real spring comes

Oliver Mellors, *Lady Chatterley's Lover* by D H Lawrence

I came down the steps and there he was at the bar before me,
So dark and so cocksure, solitary and intent,
His face inscrutable under the heavy brows, his cheekbones showing.
And he lifted his head from his drinking, and looked at me through a bellyful of remembering,
His hand on the table, loose and forgotten, like a sleeping dog.
For a moment we were together in the flood; he could have washed my soul transparent.
Then, as if a wind tossed him, he got up and came to me and I saw the black days ahead,
The complications and the ugliness and his heart as cold as cold potatoes,
And my blood sank and I did not quite dare to let him take me home.
But afterwards I regretted it, and voices in me said I had missed my chance with tenderness
And would have to light my little flame alone.

iv | How Sir Launcelot was to-fore the door of the chamber

Launcelot du Lake, *Le Morte D'Arthur*, by Thomas Malory

Before he pulled off his helm, I weened he was Sir Launcelot du Lake, a knight
wifeless and lecherous, noised to love the Queen, to take his pleasaunce with paramours
and spend his days in jousts and deeds of arms, putting better kemps than he to flight.
And yet he proffered me courtesy and gentleness and promised to fulfil all my desires
and intents. Nay, truly he seemed the flower of all men. Our chamber richly dight,
said he, 'Fair Damosel, I am no ravisher of women, nor foul churl who doth shame
to my order. As I am true knight of the Table Round, I had liefer die than grieve
you.' So saying, his helm he laid under his head and rested him long with play and game.
Yea, on my very life I would have let him wield me, yet he had lust to sleep perforce
and when day shone, made I great sorrow and was passing heavy as he took his leave
for I was ready to go with him wherever he would have me, but alas I had no horse.

v | We are not meant for happiness

Maxim de Winter, *Rebecca* by Daphne du Maurier

Two slices of bread and butter each, and China tea,
a snowy cloth, gingerbread, floury scones, crumpets
melting in the mouth, a little table drawn before the fire.
He smoked, I ate. Women are not like men, we take
our chances when we can. He stared at me moodily
wrapped in his secret self. Oh, that dark, lost look of his,
those wounded eyes, the face swept cold and clean.
He belonged in a different century, in a walled city
with winding streets and twisted spires. His cigarettes
told a smouldering truth. I sliced more angel cake.
He seized the ashtray, stubbing out desire.

vi | On ne peut croire ce qui ne se comprend pas

Pierre Abélard, *Letters of Abelard and Heloise* by Pierre Bayle

I would not have suspected him for a doctor by his dress
though who can resist the brilliance of a man whose faculties
confound the learned of his age? His person is advantageous

enough; he is formidable in logic and his conversation displays
the precepts of Ovid and the weapons of dialectic. His genius
attracts my vanity. Even the most trivial of his verses
will last as long as there are lovers in this world. Were I his mistress
he would raise me to the character of a goddess, yet (I confess
my inconsistency without a blush) it is sometimes dangerous
to have too much merit. He doats on solitude and difficulties,
his chalice holds a bitter draught. I have no use for such austerities.

vii | The only cause he knows

Rhett Butler, *Gone with the Wind* by Margaret Mitchell

In he strides, lips curled, black boots flashing - hot yam,
I'm in love! Moths in my gut, knots in my throat, all at sea
on a tide of tongues. He's swarthy as a pirate, varmint eyes, floppy
fringe, tomcat grin, cool way with a pork rib, and soon drammed
up on Southern Comfort. I swallow all his riddles with sweet tea.
Beneath the scars he claims he's soft as a shimmy, soppy
about ponies and puppies, squishy to the core, proud to wheel a pram.
He swears he'll set me up in Maryland or Tennessee,
revamp my life with barbecues and cotton. O Mammy, what a ham!
It wouldn't last. He'll always be a wham-bam-
thank-you man. I'll never be persuaded that he gives a damn.

viii | A little chapter, in which is contained a little incident

Tom Jones, *Tom Jones* by Henry Fielding

He accosted me with some of the ordinary forms of salutation, which I in the same manner
returned and our conversation began on the delicious beauty of the fine house and land.

Before we proceeded farther, he acquainted me that he intended to digress as often as he saw occasion,
assuring me there would be nothing in his demeanour inconsistent with the strictest rules of decency.

He had little sobriety in his countenance, and a propensity to many vices,
yet bad as he was, he must serve as the heroe of this history.

We walked forth on the terrace and our talk past swiftly to matters of a differ-
ent kind from those preceding: despite the virtuous love he bore another,

he claimed I had taken his heart by surprize and the rest of his body had a right to follow.

Reader, take care: nothing is more irksome than to be at one's own
expense the object of an honest man's pleasure.

Both his looks and his voice were full of tenderness, and he produced extravagant effects
augmented by wine, then, laying aside all allegory, he snatched and kissed my hand.

You may see that his nature was as difficult to be met with as a sausage from Bologna, yet, though his
animal spirits may be condemned, by some, as unnatural, my business is only to record the truth.

Therefore, lest anything offend in the perusal, I am obliged to
choak my reflections and contemplate the weather.

Suffice to say, the evening breeze was sweet, but he had led me to the top of a hill,
and how to get me down without breaking my neck, he knew not. However defi-
cient in outward tokens of respect, he was such a pretty young fellow

I gladly feasted at his table of love, and afterwards we slid down together.

CELEBRATING
Christopher Middleton
1926–2015

On the Gift of a Sea-Shell

Chrisopher Middleton

1.

They seldom say that God
Inclined his ear
To the cries of old men
From shaky patio chairs
When the Syrian military began
To shell their Aleppo souk.

And God's ear, they do say, could discern
Helen's footstep when
Sad at heart she came into sight
And on their bench of stone
As if copying spiny grasshoppers,
Sensing the heat again
The old men stopped their chirping.

2.

weil
Ohne Halt verstandlos Gott ist.
– Hölderlin

That in his young mouth he could taste
Barefoot among the ferns on his patrol
Blackberries picked from the clusters
      Behind thorn stockades, tasted
      On them the savour of salt for soon
      There was the sea, the reef to explore,
And that his tent, nights, caught whispers
From the stream it was pitched beside,
He has given me warmly thanks.

3.

Brooding under the spell of language
Reckoning on bias in our attributions,
We know it was not Homer but Chapman
Who found that grasshoppers were spiny.
Wing-case and shank for a moment in mid-air,
Then touch flitted, ear was prickled,
And the right word was there.

4.

There was no rosy sanctuary for the shell
But a cavern of antiquity and its messages.
Into a hole in the wall the shell fits
And at the back of it a winding trail begins
To traverse century after century.
Once in a while I listen there
For Helen's voice. Papyrus, parchment,
Rag-paper, none has a trace of it. Hear now
The public voices howl nasally onscreen;
Sounds like hers fell through cracks in history.
Was her accent ever judged incompatible
With her radiance? When she spoke, some people
Only tried to catch a glimpse of her tongue.

Out of the sea-shell, no perpetual murmur;
Is beauty, as a rule, like deity free but latent?
Of a rare harmony circling Kekova Achim told me:
Poignant dialogue with a finch, let it go,
A condor will call, today will have come
Bringing to the island someone who can still
Speak as she spoke, sing, imaginably, like Helen.

Drew Milne
Noisemakers of Now: Christopher
Middleton's later poems

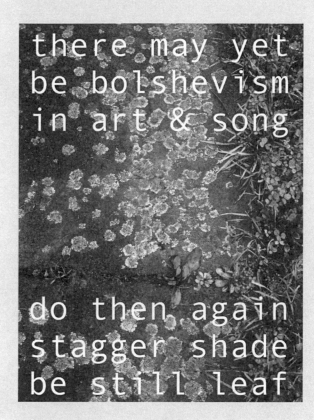

Christopher Middleton's poetry is self-evidently
and knowingly modernist, finding space for itself,
as he puts it, 'somewhere in between Brecht and
Mallarmé'.[1] Evoking familiar adjectival spectres
leaves open which of the many cloudy modern-
isms – high, low, post or neo – might best put
some pressure on the characteristics of his poetry
and poetics. A touch of Dada and Oulipo here, a
bit of Rilke or Trakl there, some Kafkaesque wit,
homages to Bruno Schulz and Robert Walser,
even a soupçon of Eliotic metaphysical wit
and gravitas for the road? It won't do and the
demon of analogy won't come out to play. There
is no question that Middleton's poetry has its
own singularity. Over a sustained body of work,
his poems offer a persistent quality that runs
amok with any conventional notion of the poet
having a distinctive voice, developing instead
a repertoire of surprises and détournements.
His characteristic syntax is agile and flexible, a
determined Yeatsian muscularity of connections
across lineation, rather than anything too parat-
actic or elusive. Working out how to read one of
Middleton's poems, however, does not provide
the reader with a code, syntactic repertoire or
signature matrix of tropes with which to crack
the rest: the singularity of each poem remains
sovereign, and this perhaps suggests why

criticism of Middleton's poetry remains sketchy
and introductory.

There is, nevertheless, a question that Middleton
shares with the more general force of modernism,
a question at odds with the prevailing provincial
domesticity of English verse, namely the ques-
tion of poetry's continuing historical veracity, its
capacity to transcend mere reportage or domestic
anecdote and make particular claims to histor-
ical truth. This question could be characterised
as an itch for transcendence, some spirituality
that would turn poetry into an ersatz religiosity.
Middleton's poetry takes pains not to delete
spirituality, resisting the temptations of a crude
Brechtian materialism that would reduce every
last iota of metaphysical experience to a mere
sign. How many contemporary poets can carry off
the appearance of being so free of god-bothering
spiritual tendencies, while nevertheless risking
such flourishes as:

On earth, in heaven, a choice of Paradises.
Isles of the Blest, Tai Shan, Immortals
tiptoe through the aura and float down,
later to ride back up again, task completed,
on snow-white deer with antlers of spidery jade.[2]

Although entitled 'Thrones', presumably as a
nod to Ezra Pound, it is not Pound but Mallarmé
that stands in as the patron saint for the pull of
poetic radiance and a knowingly philosophical
and almost Hegelian speculative tendency in
Middleton's writing. The question of spirit is
kept in play, however, not through messianic or
angelic hopes for redemption, or indeed through
hermetic avant-garde puzzles of over-heated
extremity, but through a kind of worldly tenacity
that finds abiding analogues: in birdsong; or
in the arts, notably painting, music and dance;
or in the work of other poets and writers.

One mark of this worldly tenacity is the refer-
entiality of the proper name in his poems. The
first poem of Middleton's *Collected Later Poems,*
to take a scene-setting example, is entitled 'For
Preface a Lacuna'. The poem 'refers' to the shoes
of Saint Francis, one 'Fotis', a 'Lucius' who 'was an
ass', along with the Pope and Allah, all the while
taking as a pivot, the evocation of how 'Hafis drank
in Shiraz with a demon.' The poem concludes:

Wait one moment, birds. Look, look into this.
Then tweeting, agile, out of the fresco flit.

(*CLP*, p. 3)

Birds are the ever-present companion species of
Middleton's later poems, a positively open-house
aviary of imaginative muses and ecological soli-
darity. This poem appeared in the 2007 collection
The Tenor on Horseback, contemporaneous with the
founding of Twitter, so future historicists might
need to be told that there is no joke here about
birds and the twitterati. Middleton's poetics of

1 Christopher Middleton, *Palavers & A Nocturnal Journal*
(Exeter: Shearsman, 2004), p. 29.

2 Christopher Middleton, *Collected Later Poems* (Manchester:
Carcanet, 2014), p. 258. References hereafter abbreviated in
the main text to *CLP* and page number.

'tweeting' is Twitter-free. Better references can be supplied for this lacuna. One such is that the otherwise beguiling title *The Tenor on Horseback* can be read back into the illustrious career of Gene Autry, one singing cowboy movie star of the 1930s, invoked in Alva Johnston's article 'Tenor on Horseback' (1939) in the *Saturday Evening Post.*[3] Then again, perhaps the key reference is to Matt Sprague's pulp fiction western *Tenor on Horseback* (1945), that was itself perhaps influenced by Alva Johnston. The thought that pulp fiction might be repurposed by Texan neo-modernist classicism rather gives the scholarly edge to Sprague as echt source. More likely, Middleton glimpsed the resonance of the title, imagined it shorn of its seemingly lame contextualisation, and so asks for a different sense of the 'high note in action and in music when things go haywire.' The demon with which Hafis drank is perhaps Mallarmé's demon of the analogy. One imagines, after some amateur browsing, that the poem's reference to the shoes of Saint Francis owes something to the experience of encountering said relic shoes in the vicinity of *Basilica Papale di San Francesco*, as if the attention had been caught by footwear rather than the tourist trap of frescoes. Lucius as ass suggests *The Metamorphoses* of Apuleius, more familiarly known, after St Augustine, as *The Golden Ass*. The Hafis of the poem is, one presumes, the great Persian poet Khwāja Shams-ud-Dīn Muḥammad Ḥāfeẓ-e Shīrāzī, a.k.a. Hafiz and Hafez, rather than a more contemporary friend of Middleton with a taste for a bottle of Shiraz. In short, the good folk at Google have their work cut out to keep up with the matrix of references. Readers of Middleton nevertheless learn to trust that there is some experienced specificity at work, some *trace* of the real, if not a documentary report on the significance of the names in play. It is not that Middleton would go along with Auden's quip about poetry being a clear expression of mixed feelings. The force, instead, is that of experience coming through poetic filters to offer up an artefact, a made song that aspires to radiant realism rather than experiential anecdote fluffed up in the study.

Understood accordingly, the burden of reference owes something to the fragments of world culture assembled in Ezra Pound's *Cantos*, but with a kind of pragmatic urbanity that is less judgmental or doctrinal, more surprised and surprising. Middleton's compass is serendipitous and brief, anything but epic and more prone to a debunking scepticism that prefers to respect spiritual interests over choosing to escape into prosaic satire or surrealist rhapsody. It is a difficult middle ground to occupy, and the frequent invocation of people and places helps to anchor the poetic argument in referentiality, a symbolism that persists with referentiality rather than gambling on the speculative song of paratactial implication. In the world before internet reference engines, such referentiality might have appeared 'difficult', 'obscure' or even – cue drum role of democratic opprobrium

3 *The Country Music Reader*, ed. Travis D. Stimeling (Oxford: Oxford University Press, 2015).

– *academic*. Now that the algorithms of digital culture have given the lie to such appearances, putting so many kinds of referentiality and images at our digital finger tips, the difficulty has become instead the very ease with which reference can be made. It is possible to bring up a photograph of something resembling the shoes of Saint Francis without much effort from TripAdvisor, or to track down a quick guide to the poetry of Hafis, even to read translations of Hafez by Basil Bunting. All of which reveals the extent to which the real difficulty is not referential information but the quality of the analogy and poetic argument suggested.

Anyone reading Middleton's *Collected Later Poems* is offered an extensive range of perspectives through which to reconsider cultural history and a variety of poetic analogues. A poem such as 'Orbiana' takes the reader into a Browningesque dramatic monologue that revisits scenes from the life of Barbia Orbiana, an Augusta, sometime wife of Emperor Severus Alexander, and widely known and represented for her beauty in the third century CE. Who knew? It isn't immediately evident whether Middleton expects his readers to have such information at their fingertips and now to hold it to their hearts, but the more likely implication is some encounter with a surviving representation of Orbiana that has prompted Middleton's speculative imagination to try accounting for some persisting artistic purpose and pleasure. Even readers with more than a nodding acquaintance of the contexts associated with Mallarmé are unlikely to experience Middleton's poem 'Imagine Mallarmé' as a test of their general knowledge:

Imagine Mallarmé with a long and vaporous
Periphrasis buttonholing, at his desk, the mayor
Of Mézy-sur-Seine in 1890, imploring him
To rid the neighbourhood of a herd of pigs,
Which he politely called, of course, *messieurs*.

(*CLP*, p. 19)

Imaginative reconstruction of the contextual ecology of significant artistic practice is more evidently the burden of the poem's argument, which concludes:

Oink oink in the distance, Mallarmé declared,
His painting luminous across his knees
While the carriole jogged through the twilight:
*It makes me happy, just to think now
I'm living in the same age as Monet.*

(*CLP*, p. 19)

Middleton teases out the imaginative difference – are *we* still in the same age as Monet, and if not, finding in Mallarmé a cultural exemplum, what might we in our age be doing about resuscitating the dead arts, to say nothing of our analogous contributions to the politics of pig-farming. Middleton in this sense is a decisively referential poet, offering not allusions but concretely imagined instances, moments, works of art and their contexts. He is not, however, an academic poet, nor, in the end, a poet offering to shore up fragments from world culture amid the ruins. The range of reference suggests instead a poet engaged in reading, responding to art and the world around him, and thinking through processes of artistic research as a poet and translator rather than as a scholar. His poems are not afraid to evoke, juxtapose and dance across a matrix of referentiality that owe a good deal to Middleton's own sense of cultural priorities and tastes. We are invited to participate in an intelligent conversation rather than worship at the shrine of his chosen relics. Extending his imaginative reconstruction into new recognitions of the agricultural and social contexts sustaining artistic environments makes it clear too that this conversation involves more than fetishising historical artefacts, implicating his poetics instead in a historical ecology of art and aesthetic perception.

In a poem entitled 'A Difference of Degree', the second of *Eleven Canticles* from his collection *Just Look at the Dancers* (2012), Middleton offers an elegy for the passing of monarchs. Not, that is, the human variety, but, rather, the monarch butterfly, perceived in its migrations between North America and Mexico:

Where thousands flocked, age after age,
now you might see just one or two.

The doctored farms to north and south
made for the migrants an unfavourable fare.

Neighbour, you might have noticed nothing.
Neighbour, by this we are diminished also.

(*CLP*, p. 230)

Middleton is not pre-eminently a poet of nature, some kind of latter-day eco-sophist. It is nevertheless a mark of his concrete attention to noticing how the world goes, that the fate of Mexican migration through Texas is here given an ecological frame. The contemporary urgency involved in ecological recognition could be traced back through Ruskin's storm-cloud of the nineteenth century into the romantic perceptions of natural history. Middleton's more characteristic tone is one of Horatian urbanity metamorphosed through French and German modernism. A classicist modernist lament is glimpsed here in the sense that it is possible to remark from a higher perspective that 'we' are diminished, claiming nevertheless some higher, but rather rootless élan that might resist such diminishment.

There is frequently a felt pressure of political and ecological change in Middleton's poetry, often articulated with a movingly steely resistance to the temptation to false pathos or emotional escapism. As his poem 'On the Futility of Pathos' pithily notes: 'oppression sucks' (*CLP*, p. 359). There is also a sense that contemporaneity, for Middleton, offers a rather diminished, even fallen sense of perspective. The conflict between contemporary urbanity and a Poundian rummaging through different historical cultures motivates the drama and tension of many of his poems. There

are moments – as when, in 'Homage to Alkan', Middleton writes, 'I'm walking out in 1865 or so' – that rather invite the response, *come off it, no you are not, you're a twenty-first century poet writing a poem that leans rather heavily on our historical imagination*. The historical personae are nevertheless not, in the main, those of Browningesque dramatic monologues, but closer to a more persistently personal mediation, more akin to W.B. Yeats or W.H. Auden, offering personally inflected mediation of imaginative materials. Middleton cherishes his chosen materials as significant cultural touchstones that he seeks to rework for a more persistent and undiminished sense of contemporaneity.

Evidently at home in the imaginative worlds of Hölderlin, Mallarmé, Trakl and Rilke, but also in European and Arabic culture more generally, there is then something surprisingly jarring about encountering Raphael Nadal, the Spanish 'king' of clay-court tennis, in a poem by Middleton entitled 'Against Frenzy':

In a singlet costumed, sailor pants,
Elvis of tennis, the baboon Nadal
Has fired off a winning shot and whirls,
Exhibiting his muscled butt, punching up through air
A phallic fist. My, see his prance,
When millions roar, watching him hit

With malice, bodily this it is
Degrades his art, in ostentation of it,
Degrades his public, now vomiting applause –

(*CLP*, p. 34)

This harsh Olympian judgment – 'bodily this it is' – has no truck with some Pindaric imperative to produce laureate odes honouring sporting heroes. The violence of calling Nadal a 'baboon' is more than 'snootily' and politically incorrect, a violence more reminiscent of Wyndham Lewis than Jonathan Swift. The suggestion that the arts and public culture are thus degraded from some former, higher quality comes with the full weight of that patrician modernist disgust exemplified by Adorno's critique of the culture industry. But as Adorno also quipped, a critic can hardly make such criticisms without claiming to have the culture that culture lacks. Even if there is something troubling about Nadal's air-punching, something that disquiets gentlemanly aestheticians of tennis, why pick out Nadal for such dark opprobrium, and what motivates the bestial characterisation of the millions that roar and vomit?

Such moments are not characteristic of Middleton's poetry, indeed something is strikingly awry here, as if an unguardedly felt irritation has gone unedited. There is, nevertheless, a muscular retort to contemporary 'mass', or 'popular' culture running through Middleton's later poems. In 'Update on the Phrygian Mode', for example, Middleton writes that:

Swinish screams combine with a deafening
Blast of strings picked with electricity,

Flogged bar after bar the same dull beat,
Smeared with drool the stereotypical words

(*CLP*, p. 117)

The object of this spleen remains unnamed,
loosely characterised as if 'we' would recognise
the general phenomenon, and the critique is
hardly subtle:

Reiterating antique measures that you trash,
What might you make of this,
Noisemakers of now? Unless you go with the flow
Down the drain, kiss goodbye to money.

(*CLP*, p. 164)

This pathology of contemporary noise is offset
in Middleton's poetry by the evocation not just
of an alternative sense of modernist tradition
and its fragments of 'truer' culture, but also by
a continual attention to the persistent noise and
song of birds: 'there is beauty in birds and all
about them' (*CLP,* p. 85). Against the summary
judgment of our culture – 'Now brutish live music
deadens a multitude of minds.' (*CLP*, p. 276) –
Middleton counterposes a neo-classical poetic
that Matthew Arnold might have warmed to:

Early Greeks, quite at home
with gods they had to wrestle with

Dynasties brawled, the primal rapture
sparked a thought of civil freedom

From one of them the peacock rose,
Music to worship by, and mania

Human waste, the stink of it,
Achieved a gusto in their speech

(*CLP*, p. 352)

Perhaps because such untimely meditations on
the fate of western culture are unfashionable
and difficult to ground in contemporary culture,
Middleton's points of reference rarely engage
with contemporary culture much beyond the
aftermath of the Second World War. Indeed,
the sequence of poems entitled 'During The
Aftermath' is one of Middleton's most successful
cultural challenges, posing an array of questions
as to the continuing significance of the 1940s,
both for his personal experience and for world
culture. Many of Middleton's poems evoke the
England and Europe of the 1930s and 1940s as
cultural pivots, the youth of both the poet and
of subsequent culture. Perhaps because the
critical vantage from which an often damning
cultural balance sheet is drawn up is somewhat
deracinated, rather too insistently retrospective,
Middleton also evokes the fragile ecology of
non-human life:

    The thousand songs
That rush from the birds when Spring

is what they feel – what life
what future might there be on earth without birdsong
        to brace, to console, to welcome us. [....]

Could I ever, believing birds, have even
gone halfway only with Paul Celan? Since when
        did a new coherence between
ourselves and undivided nature
cease to be thinkable?

(*CLP*, p. 86)

In the context of what has recently been called
'anthropocene lyric',[4] various answers suggest
themselves. Middleton's perspective on the politics
of ecology is more classical, almost reassuringly
conventional and urbane, rather than part of an
experimental journey into deep ecology. Once
his interest in birdscapes is noticed, however, the
question of birds and birdsong can be seen as
providing an underlying ecology of perception –
species companionship and shared environments
– in many of his later poems. There are a number
of poems that represent avian kind, and a number
of poems in which birds flit in and out without
becoming subjects exactly. Indeed, Middleton's
ecological tendency resists anthropomorphising
birds too quickly: they remain estranged friends
rather than feathered messengers. In *A Keeper of
the Reliquary*, more or less the poem that closes
his *Collected Later Poems*, Middleton conjures
Rilke, Malatesta's phantom, and Laforgue before
concluding with an evocation of J. Alfred Prufrock:

        First heard
one hundred years ago today the unsteady voice
dispelled a miasma of hushed bombast and pulverised
the gum then sugaring lyric speech in England

(*CLP*, p. 378)

But the ecological dérive Middleton deploys to
conclude this homage to T.S. Eliot offers a displace-
ment from Parisian poetics into a rather curious
environment:

galleries emptied fill with fat bamboo
goblins riot round the hob but on the porch
there is a free man who talks with the fireflies.

(*CLP*, p. 379)

There is, as so often in Middleton's poems,
a considered and playful turning away from
anything quite settled or predictable – why 'fat'
bamboo and hob goblins? – as if Middleton's
poetics necessarily offsets its muscular syntax
with a kind of playful nonsense, non-sequiturs
or Dadaist fun puns, a quality of whimsy that
struggles to resist the more decadent charms of
a mode better exemplified by Wallace Stevens.
This ongoing struggle with 'the exorbitant, the
bizarre, the obscurely angelic' perhaps explains

4 Thomas Bristow, *The Anthropocene Lyric: An Affective
Geography of Poetry, Person, Place* (London: Palgrave
Macmillan, 2015).

Middleton's distaste with his first two collections, and the early influence of what he calls 'the lackadaisically florid Nicholas Moore'.[5] Middleton turned against the nevertheless likeable but sadly neglected poetics of Nicholas Moore. This schools his own poetics in a sceptical stringency in the face of anything wildly romantic or florid, sometimes to the extent of foregrounding an anti-poetic tone that owes something to the assault on mid-century 'apocalyptic' and modernist poetics. Middleton never succumbed to the full impact of Movement orthodoxy, but now that such orthodoxy has become merely historical it is possible to see that Middleton's poetics sought its own distance from the perceived excesses of the new apocalypse and all that sailed in it. Despite his perception of the diminishing returns of contemporary culture there is nevertheless more to the possibility of noisemaking now than Middleton allows into his poetry. His inventively deracinated urbanity nevertheless offers a persistently intelligent, various and wittily sceptical modernist poetics that sustains interest through the remarkable range of his later work.

5 Christopher Middleton, *Palavers & A Nocturnal Journal* (Exeter: Shearsman, 2004), p. 29.

Spring Poem for Christopher Middleton
Stanley Moss

1.
It's Monday, I phone. You answer, coughing, whisper:
'My doctor says two days and I'll be dead.
I'm afraid of falling off the bed into my grave' –
that means to me a couple of twists
of the screwdriver or monkey wrench
and you'll become unintelligibly human.

My mind is a waterbug. I write chatter... Life and death
are unhappy lovers. Is there a marriage,
is life the bride or bridegroom?
How many times can a father give the bride away?
Do life and death create a nation, like the marriage
of Fernando and Isabella – death Aragon, life Castille?
No reason, there are always the disasters of war.
Dear friend, *death is part of life* doesn't work for me.
I prefer *the end is part of the play*.

Actors and gentles, there is a change of decorum,
a grave eccentricity performed in an O.
It is winter. The sun is like a slum.
Without a bone, your frightened dog
already shakes at the stench
of your death. Without philosophy
he licks your face and feet
in hope of resurrection. A winter passion,
your life is disrobed before the public,
you are denied another Sabbath for no reason.
It should displease the Lord – this passing on
we know nothing of. I do not say the beads.
I pray there is a God of love who reads.

2.
Ten winter days have passed. I phone.
I'm certain telephones don't ring
in Heaven, Hell, or Purgatory.
You answer, 'Hello... the crisis is over.
Now my neurosurgeon says I have some time,
a day or two, a month, you never know,
...my handwriting is very shaky.' Hurrah,
it's March, there's reason to hope you'll see
Texas summer corn, roses in Westminster in April.
Soon, I'll send you this poem for a laugh.
Metaphor and reality have not come together.
I invented your good dog,
a gift to keep you from loneliness.

3.
(Is it better that the dead are buried
or go up in flames in clean clothes?)
In your poetry, you write under oath
not to treat as a thing of the mind
things that are of the mind only.
After their jealousy and lovemaking,
beauty and truth marry at the local registry,
take the vows of all religions,
or just have a long affair. I toast 'To life!'
Christopher, brush away death by failing heart;
better Zeus, on a distant evening,
when you are surrounded by love,
ground you with a thunderbolt.
A hundred years!... Christopher died yesterday.
Metaphor and reality have come together.

John Clegg
If there was a snake here, I'd apologise: Middleton's 'Coral Snake' & D.H. Lawrence

I wonder if two great poems have ever had as close a relationship as D.H. Lawrence's 'Snake' and Christopher Middleton's 'Coral Snake'. By 'close' I don't mean 'dependent'; that would leave 'Coral Snake' subservient, and where there's the possibility of a comparison I slightly prefer Middleton's poem. I mean winding together, like the double-helical spiral staircases I saw in Santiago de Compostela. Reaching out and over the banister is enough to bridge the gap between the two, but it's a trick – you're not close at all, if you want to join someone on the other staircase you have to run back down and start again from the bottom.

I think the two poems can achieve something like this because snake-lore is such a tangle of compelling and competing intuitions (not all of which are specifically cultural: macaque monkeys raised in captivity are particularly distressed by images of snakes, although they've never been exposed to them in the wild). Our positive obligations towards other animals are uncomplicated, or at least undertheorised, and Middleton writes particularly well about creatures that can look after themselves: one would be ill-advised to disturb his tarantula ('don't anyone / dare come'), or his kangaroo ('If it comes too close for comfort, / You run'). But snakes carry with them a conflicting obligation in the observer, one towards wider human society, both explicit and intuitive, as in Lawrence:

The voice of my education said to me
He must be killed,
For in Sicily the black, black snakes are innocent, the
                              gold are venomous.

And voices in me said, If you were a man
You would take a stick and break him now, and finish
                              him off.

And this reaction is predictable enough in itself to become part of Middleton's response, as he sees the lethal coral snake slithering over his vegetable patch:

He had come out of nowhere like evil.
He didn't care about me or want me.
I cared about him enough – it was fear.

Fear not for me, no, but for him, the snake:
Long-trapped, an old horror breaks loose,
Later you say Alas, the snake was beautiful.
So I wonder what I can kill him with,
And notice in my hand the hoe...

Middleton can pre-empt Lawrence, can recognise through Lawrence the danger in his stock responses. But the voices go unanswered in

Lawrence ('He must be killed', they demand, but Lawrence's snake gets away), and the voices in Middleton which include Lawrence himself will likewise go unanswered. 'Long-trapped, an old horror breaks loose'; the ancestral fear of snakes is itself figured as a snake (Middleton is about to trap the real snake under the blade of the hoe), a metaphor which eats its own tail, and resolves into a terrifying unlogic: 'So I wonder what I can kill him with...'

That word 'horror' is the same word which eventually provokes Lawrence into his own violent flounce: 'A sort of horror, a sort of protest against his withdrawing into that horrid black hole, / [...] Overcame me now his back was turned'. When we read Lawrence in school this line did not impress us very much: he had been pitched to the class as a great observer of nature, whose attention compensated for the prosiness of his language, and here he was giving us a snake which could turn his back – could turn his back as he slithered into a hole, no less – hot on the tail of the equally ludicrous 'snake-easing his shoulders'.

What I think Lawrence was getting at is the same effect Middleton achieves, as he presses down on the hoe and crushes the snake's head:

I didn't want it to be done, I didn't.
But how now to stop, considering his pursuits,
Easygoing as he is, pinheaded, slow to bite –

They say his tooth sits so far back
He needs to chew to do you in.

For there was more snake now in me than him.

Lawrence's snake can 'turn his back' because he's being deliberately anthropomorphised and filled with human dignity. (Simultaneously, the word 'human' is itself being emptied of dignity: as in 'my accursed human education'.) But Lawrence's effect is achieved bluntly, almost ridiculously; Middleton's counter-effect, as man becomes snake, is subtler.

For instance, the internal rhymes in the middle section of the quotation (tooth, chew, do, you) have a chewiness of their own: they make the reader get their own teeth in. More important are the double meanings: here, 'pursuits' (both the range the snake is prepared to chase an attacker, and his sympathetic habits or occupations), and elsewhere: '...if I shift the hoe / He'll streak through the chicken wire and I'll be / Cut off.' (If Middleton continues to press down the hoe, of course, the roles will be reversed.) And more important still is that 'considering', as he rifles through his mental information about the species of snake – finding to his unease that all the things he remembers are reasons to stop, not to press on: 'He's mellow, he's stupid, and anyway he isn't really dangerous' – until he thinks of the horrible fact about the teeth, and is glad to have thought of it, because he has already committed himself.

(I've never come across a venomous snake in the wild, but walking across Hampstead Heath the other morning I saw a rat on a bare patch of ground behind a stump, frozen in terror looking straight at me. I bent almost unconsciously for a stone, and as I considered for a moment whether or not to throw it, I remembered something I'd read about how many stomach ulcers rats got from the stress of living among humans, and how some of them made two-hour commutes, and at the same time felt my small sympathy to be an imposition or an obstruction of some natural process, that I should throw the stone and not listen to these voices. I think both Middleton and Lawrence are astute on the psychology here.)

In an interview with Marius Kociejowski (*Palavers & A Nocturnal Journal*, Shearsman 2004), Middleton settles on 'hi-falutin' as his central reservation about Lawrence's poetic diction. 'Coral Snake' can itself abut or skirt the hi-falutin:

I could not do it, not to him, looking so
True to himself, making his wisdom tell,
It shot through me quicker than his poison would:
The glory of his form, delicate organism,
Not small any more, but raw now, and cleaving,
Right there, to the bare bone of creation.

And so I gripped the second stone but steadily
Thumped that telling head down flat [...]

Or rather, hi-falutinness is what one might detect on a first reading, especially in the very Lawrentian chain of abstracts: 'wisdom', 'glory', 'creation'. It is only as the passage clarifies in the mind that one picks up the register, the Edenic notes carefully insinuated. 'The bare bone of creation': the bone closest in shape to a snake, of course, is the rib, and in the metaphor we are surely meant to remember the creation of Eve – and the snake in Eden, whose best offer was also 'wisdom'. 'Cleaving' is a pun which sends us in two directions at once, like 'Cut off' earlier; 'the bare bone of creation' is rather an opening of possibilities. (For instance, the bone-dry Texan soil, the bone's curve insinuating the curve of the earth, and the whole metaphor working to make the snake suddenly enormous.)

Both poems by necessity move into pathos for their endings. Lawrence is characteristically good on the psychology here:

And I thought of the albatross
And I wished he would come back, my snake.

Coleridge's albatross is not, of course, a relevant thing to be thinking of (and in any case the Mariner's motives for shooting the bird are not clear; Empson believed it was to make soup out of). But it's exactly the comparison which would occur to somebody wishing to invest their petty action with a dark dignity, and the second line, with its unconsciously patronising possessive ('*my* snake'), is just as well-observed.

Lawrence has lost the snake and fails to recapture him: Middleton has killed the snake and fails to preserve it.

    The colours
Now have faded; having no pure alcohol,
I pickled the snake in half a pint of gin.

But the snake and its colours are, of course, preserved by the poem, 'Black, / red, and yellow rings more regular far [...] / Than wedding bands on a jeweller's ringstick', just as Lawrence's snake in the closing lines allows Lawrence the occasion for the 'expiation' he has just given us.

When I read Middleton alongside Lawrence, I think of the line from 'Tradition and the Individual Talent', the odd Escher-like spiral into which Eliot locks the living and the dead:

Some one said: 'The dead writers are remote from us because we *know* so much more than they did.' Precisely, and they are that which we know.

And I think as well of the penultimate sentence of Lawrence's 'Snake', and of the letter I would have written to Christopher Middleton. I began it I don't know how many times, and laid it aside again and again, thinking it ought to wait until I had a reason to send it, beyond the selfish desire for *contact*. And so I missed my chance with one of the lords of life.

Michael Hersch
Reflections on Christopher Middleton

... Distance perhaps
is all for the best. Sufficient for the day
are piles of ash.
          – Christopher Middleton

There are a few people whose presence in my life radically altered the path I was taking. In some cases these individuals opened my eyes to things I would not have otherwise seen; things not in my nature or things I was blind to through a lack of insight or skill, or perhaps through lack of experience or predilection. Christopher Middleton's influence on me was different. He was able to clarify for me elements of who I already was. Through his work and his friendship he gave me many things, but his greatest gift was to provide a kind of self-realization, an ability that allowed me to see facets of my nature which up until that point I did not recognise. This new-found sense of self gave me the courage to follow through with creative decisions I may not have under other circumstances made.

Though we came from vastly different backgrounds and there was between us an age difference of more than four decades, a strong connection nonetheless seemed to quickly emerge. We met in Germany. We were both fellows at the American Academy in Berlin, and early on somehow ended up in a long discussion about Friedrich Hölderlin's poem 'Hälfte des Lebens', in particular how the last line was dealt with by those translating it into English. He spent almost a half hour speaking about just a single word within that line, and the minefield that word presented when it came to its translation. Later during the conversation, when he learned that I was a composer, he expressed an interest in hearing some music. We went to an upright piano, and I played for about ninety minutes. Each time I would finish a work he would ask if I might play another. He seemed at once incredibly enthusiastic and puzzled; I remember thinking that he did not like the music. I was unsure as to why he kept wanting to hear more. Perhaps he wanted to like it, and was simply waiting for something with which he resonated. After the last piece he suddenly disappeared to his room and came back with a number of books of his poetry. He asked if I might read them.

Whether or not Christopher had reservations about my music that day, it quickly became clear that I had none about his poetry. Those poems, lines, fragments, even single words struck me with tremendous force – so much so that I had an experience which up to that point I had not encountered with any text, the feeling that I *must* engage with these words musically. The sounds that came to ear and mind were those for solo piano, but not the voice (Christopher found this interesting as he assumed I would be thinking along the lines of setting his words for a singer). The reason I was thinking instrumentally rather than vocally was that I could not imagine then that the perfection the words achieved on the page could be transmitted to another medium. I even preferred their existence on the page to Christopher's own reading of them (though I never told him that). They functioned for me something like ignition points. They were inspiration, but more than that they felt like companions. They still do. Christopher's words often made me feel as if he saw the world through eyes similar to my own, and consequently many of those fragments that I selected for my first work to engage with his poetry seemed to express in letters what I was attempting to say with the pitches, rhythms and silences of music. Like much great art, Christopher's work makes people feel less alone in the world. It certainly had that effect on me.

Christopher knew from the outset, and said he was comfortable with, the fact that I would be excerpting his texts for this new piece, almost never utilizing an entire poem. Yet I grew increasingly nervous that he would not approve when he saw what amounted to a libretto for an instrumental work where that libretto consisted largely of fragments of his words. Despite these reservations, I continued to write. Approximately half of the work's movements begin with his poetry. The other half, designated *intermezzi* in the score, are unconnected to any text. Though we corresponded often during the years I was composing the music, I never showed him the score of what ended up being a multi-hour fifty-movement work during that period.

In October of 2016, it will have been a decade since I gave the first performance of this piece, entitled *The Vanishing Pavilions*. It ultimately took me some four years to write the music and another year to prepare it for performance. When Christopher arrived the day before the première of the work in Philadelphia, I presented him the score to look at for the first time. We sat quietly in the lobby of his hotel, Christopher scanning the early pages of the score where the selected poetry appears comprehensively before the music proper begins. He would lean forward in his chair as if to say something one moment, but would not, then he would sink back down again. I don't recall ever being as nervous as I was during the time from when he took the open score in hand to when he closed it and placed it on his lap. He proceeded to sit motionless for about a minute. He then nodded silently, gently smiled, rose, put his hand on my shoulder and thanked me. He presented me with a gift, a binder that had been his father's music folder. He hugged me (which caught me completely off guard) and we then had a drink. He didn't tell me what he thought but he seemed happy, or at least content. For a moment I forgot that I had to perform this two-and-a-half-hour piece in fewer than twenty-four hours. And in that moment I forgot about everything except how lucky I was to have been afforded this friendship and collaboration. I have felt this way about my relationship with Christopher ever since. He was a gift.

Christopher's generosity of spirit was as immense as the world his poetry encompassed. I've written before that what he could convey in a fragment of poetry I still am attempting to achieve in music. Soon after we met, the attacks of 11 September, 2001 occurred. People in the community where we lived were horrified, frightened, angry, disbelieving – I among them. It was strange for me to be so far from the U.S. during that chaotic moment in history. One morning during that autumn Christopher came into the dining area where I was sitting alone and asked how I was doing – how people I knew in New York and Washington were doing, but more importantly what I was working on. He asked if I was writing music. I said, 'Yes.' I was completing my second symphony at the time. He said, 'Good. I'm going to write some poems.' He then turned and went back to his room.

Thomas Lowenstein
On Christopher Middleton

A shortened version of an essay published in The Bow Wow Shop *in March 2014, this version takes off from a brief account of English poetry in the 1950s and continues here with the innovative publication of* Torse 3.

. . . Most arresting was the appearance of Christopher Middleton's *Torse 3* (Longmans 1962, and a US edition from Harcourt, Brace and World – a triplet of nouns whose comic dissonance can't have been lost on the poet).

The title, *Torse 3,* was also the epigraph to the volume and stood both as a found poem and an indication of method. 'Torse 3' *qua* quotation was also an erudite device, a lexical *koan* suggesting a subtly differentiating vision that emerges from the columns of a reference book:

Not (implied) torse 1, 'the crested band or wreath by which the crest is joined to the helmet.'
Nor torse 2 (implied further of course) = 'TORSO'.
But torse 3, 'a developable surface; a surface generated by a moving straight line which at every instant is turning, in some plane or other through it, about some point or other in its length.'

Surprisingly, this term, from *torquere,* 'to twist', was relatively recent, having had a second airing, before Christopher's third, in the *Encyclopedia Britannica,* 1879 where the poet found it.

To the reader of the early sixties, this third citation becomes a quiddity, a pantomimic lazzo, from whose knot derives the development of a line which had started to unwind in the previous century: the years in which the poet's elders had been born and from which this least Victorian of individuals had, by 1960, already travelled a long distance to befriend us with the mobility of his intelligence and teach us to be happy and inquisitive people.

To extract myself from this knot, I would merely suggest that while we English havered uncomfortably between choices that were arriving from the safe territories of the Movement poets whose dialects we could either repudiate or try mimicking (though Prynne and Roy Fisher were forging their own ideolects), Christopher had already been ranging through Europe and America, at work beyond Anglophone boundaries, and for him experiment and tradition were no longer antinomies. He had long absorbed the vast experiential latitudes of Goethe and of German romanticism. Hölderlin and Mörike were familiars. The Expressionists and August Stramm (whose 'nonsequences', to borrow a Middleton title, prefigure Celan's syntax), pan-European Dada and surrealism were lived history. Modernism, in the German canon in which Christopher had long been immersed, after all, had arrived abruptly in the early nineteenth

century with Büchner's *Danton, Lenz* and *Woyzeck.* And so while in the UK these worlds might be apprehended as quasi-ethnographic data, this had long been where Christopher had read and exercised imagination. It is, for example, a mark of his identification with these European worlds that his translations of Robert Walser both brought that writer to Anglophone readers and, via a celebrated paper, introduced Walser to a wider German readership. 'The admirable Christopher Middleton', wrote Susan Sontag in her preface to a Carcanet edition. A welcome, if faint, signal.

Reverting to *Torse 3*, the 'Definition' as Christopher headed his epigraph, perhaps provides a way into that major volume, and even to some of the subsequent thirteen books which make up his *Collected Poems*.

Four elements may be identified in that epigraph. First, there is the straight line. Second, a 'developable surface'. Third is the movement of both line and surface. And fourth are the planes through which the surface travels as it is generated by the linear axis.

Asked to what art such a definition belonged, one might hesitate between Constructivism and the Vorticism of Brzeska. Indeed, the textures and movements of Christopher's oeuvre belong not exclusively to interactions between thought and language. The musical, the visual and the architectural are as present in his work as palpably as are painting and line-drawing in the music of Debussy and Satie – whose miniatures are close, in play and brightness, to a number of Christopher's shorter pieces such as 'Irish' from *Two Horse Wagon Going By* or 'The Parrot House on Bruton Street, 1830' from *Intimate Chronicles*, or the paintings of Mondrian or Leger in which an arithmetic music lies within a flat, chromatically divided silence.

To put it crudely, Christopher's poetry, from the outset, has been one of movement, multi-textured surfaces and implied levels of signification, whose multiplicity is suggested by surface planes of fractured narrative and image as these move, often hermetically, through a contemplative development. Meaning inheres both within an accountable narrative and in juxtapositions involving the coincidence of subjectivity and impersonality, involution and exfoliation. The lovely 'Montagnola' from *Torse 3* exemplifies such junctures. Here, the aged Hermann Hesse sits stirring

with a silver spoon, his coffee backwards [...]
you could have sworn,
as he spoke to unspeak every word he spoke,
that his freedom was a way to deny nothing.
His only memorable remark was an afterthought:
a butterfly with open wings
clung alive to the minute-hand of his study clock.
He did not allude to his lyric on the subject;
and on reflection it was hard to tell if paradox
or wisdom lay, inextricably veiled,
in the churning limpid veil of his senescence.

Hesse died in summer 1962 and Christopher had visited him a year or so earlier. Here the approach to Hesse's house by 'forked paths' is decorated with changing textures of things and colours until we arrive at the depths of Hesse's alternating speech and silence, which is suddenly transected in present time by the materialization of a butterfly whose image had figured in one of Hesse's early poems.

Twists of inference are yet more clearly enacted in 'Ginestra' from *Carminalenia*:

Yellow explodes and replenishes itself,
With pulse on pulse an airy
Marine perfume floats as is
A robe of shivers around the mountain

It must be contained
In the chemical roots
Nothing explodes, the yellow simply
Unfolds; nothing,
Nevertheless, unfolds like this,
Metaphor and fact refuse to mix

And the plant hangs in such
Delicate balance the wonder is
Yellow shrank in us to a blazon
For jealousy [...]

Just as the yellow of broom on a southern coastline 'simply unfolds', so the poet demonstrates its flowering in the poem's movement.

There are poems such as 'On a Photograph of Chekhov' from *Intimate Chronicles* and the history contained in 'Lines for Jennifer' in *The Word Pavilion* that move against the current of this practice. Another narrative is 'Coral Snake', from *Apocrypha Texana*: descriptive of a manly snake-killing struggle which, in its moral ambivalence, pays homage to D.H. Lawrence. 'Coral Snake' brings a glimpse of the poet as physical being, caught between planting seed potatoes and turning his hoe on a snake. As in Lawrence, the tension lies between an obligation to human well-being and acknowledgement of the creature's independence:

He had come out of nowhere like evil.
He didn't care about me or want me.
I cared about him enough – it was fear.

Fear, not for me, no, but for him, the snake:
Long-trapped, an old horror breaks loose,
Later you say Alas, the snake was beautiful.
So I wonder what I can kill him with [...]

Reverting to Christopher's immersion in German literature, it was one thing to know that world, another to assimilate its workings and become a part of its processes. The extent of Christopher's knowledge of the German canon is best exemplified in his translations, which most tellingly are contained in the first volume of the Princeton Goethe series and the Chicago edition of Hölderlin and Mörike. Christopher's translations represent a brilliant poetic mimesis. Equally impressive are the introductory essays and mind-expanding end-notes – for example, Mörike's 'Plague in the Forest', where Christopher analyses senarius and alexandrine metres, plus citations from

Greek, *Faust*, Racine, Baudelaire, Rimbaud and Klopstock. Or *Auf eine Lampe,* in which Mörike's aesthetics, with reference to Schiller, Goethe, Novalis, Wordsworth, Theocritus and the *Timaeus,* are defined with relish and spontaneity.

As just suggested, Christopher's literary knowledge lies far beyond the Germanic. The essays in *Jackdaw Jiving* illuminate diverse and culturally non-exclusive literatures which meet through Christopher's prose in tectonically convergent arguments. These read as a super-athletics performed by a virtuoso who delights in the diversity of made objects, whether these be Viking prows, Ian Hamilton Finlay inscriptions or the poetry of Günter Eich and the other natural curiosities that his book celebrates.

'Celebration' is a lazy old word. But it is helpful in diverting us from the merely academic, because, for want of a better word, Christopher's work represents a lifetime's existential curiosity and pleasure which is most immediately expressed in an astonishing variety of titles: Memory of the Vaucluse, A Report from the Euphrates, The Cappadocian Chandelier, Pushkin and the Cat, Figure of a Chinese Drummer, Antigone's Drift... One might read such a Contents List almost as an independent poem expressed by a sensibility in touch with curiosities of the world which we would miss but for the poet's observation of them.

The pleasure is evident. And Christopher belongs to that society inhabited by poets such as Marvell, Ponge, Wallace Stevens and Williams, whose work expresses pleasure in the sensuality of things, both for their own sake and for their evocation of a world of multiplicity that impinges on us.

And Christopher's scholarship would be poetically barren were it not embodied in enjoyment. Poems, translations, essays and endnotes are communicated as part of a weave whose elements co-exist and in which we live in reciprocity. The expatriate poet is both rooted in this world and a traveller whose movement, like the jackdaw, dances and gives voice. The poet's ancestry, his Englishness, is relegated without denial. But the movement, whether it is journeys through America, Provence or Cappadocia, is never of escape, but rather of encounter. If the connections are quick they are also contemplative and (as suggested by the 'torse 3' emblem) subtly dimensioned. And in a sense this engagement is one of eroticism: an in-touchness with the inner and outer, mind and body. Such eroticism, of which sexuality is just one expression, is a mark of most important poets. And what the poet apprehends from such experience he gives back to the world with a subtle, wide-ranging and spontaneous generosity.

Marius Kociejowski
The Very Rich Hours of Christopher Middleton

So many things to be said about him, I juggle a hundred balls and, blast it all, I drop every last one of them. They, in their many colours, roll away in as many directions. So thick and fast do my memories of Christopher come that I'll have to try and push just a few of them into a narrow place. I'll begin with our telephone conversation of 21 February, 2014 when the doctors had given him just three days to live. The telephone is not the best of mediums through which to say one's final goodbyes, but the best that could be made of it was made – a conversation that was at once terrible, beautiful, and intimate. I got myself into a deeply mournful state while he, a week later, was still very much alive.

A heart apparently riddled with holes, it was still strong enough to get him through and I think I'm now at liberty to say what probably got him over that terrible hurdle: he'd fallen in love. He told me this in such a quiet whisper I had to ask him to repeat himself. 'Oh, never mind', he replied, as if clawing back something he'd said by mistake. I persisted. 'But she's *old*', he said. 'And how old would *old* be?' 'Sixty-five!', he exclaimed, as if startled by the strangeness of the number itself. 'Ah, you mean a year younger than my wife', I replied. Christopher was one of those men who couldn't bear to see the fresh milk in the wooden barrel curdle. I set against this, as did my wife who loved him, a thousand finer qualities. Old age never really got him whole. It couldn't dim the glint in his eye, the twinkle in his voice. A captive of circumstance, as he had now become, what he needed most was to love. Some weeks later, when I enquired after the lady in question, he stammered, as if mortally wounded, 'She thinks history begins with the pyramids!' She dismayed him as much as she'd revivified him. Could it be he found in her not only affection but also an unthinking world he might try to save? So fearful he was that all would collapse and, with it, the art of poetry that it became one of his perennial themes. It got so I had to avoid striking the dark note. As for the addressee of one of his late poems it was a sentimental love without any roots in the physical, but I am fairly convinced he owed his life if not to her directly then to the fact of that winter love. It was enough. It was enough to enable him to squeeze another year and three quarters of life and to write the poems, almost as if against an injunction not to, that would comprise his final collection, *Nobody's Ezekiel* (Hopewell, 2015).

We spoke every Sunday afternoon between five and six, eleven and twelve Texas time. I greatly missed his letters, of course, which were often marvellous literary exercises (although maybe 'explorations' is the better word), a mind always at work and play. I'll say it now: he was one of the great letter-writers of our age. Sooner or later, a reckoning will need to be made with them. They'll stay put when the majority of our words have vanished into cyberspace. When his eyes began to fail and writing became a chore, we agreed to communicate thenceforth by phone. Now, on a greyish Sunday afternoon, approaching five o'clock, I want for his *voice*. It was one of the most beautiful voices I've ever known to issue from a man's face – a lilting voice at once quizzical, playful, speculative and desirous of not just literature but also a decent bottle of wine, a splash of Poulenc or Mompou playing in the background and, above all, the light and colour one finds in the French paintings he so loved.

I reach for Richard McDougall's *The Very Rich Hours of Adrienne Monnier.* Did we ever discuss that book? Did Christopher not recommend it to me in the first place? There are on my shelves many books he gave me, Debussy's writings on music, a biography of that Parisian muse Misia Sert, Dilys Powell's *The Villa Ariadne*, and Marmaduke Pickthall's *The Children of the Nile*. So many of them were unexpected treasures, which was why going into second-hand bookshops with him was such fun because he was a passionate explorer of the arcane. The dullest-looking volume would come alive in his hands. Who but him sang the praises of Ferdynand Antoni Ossendowski? He'd greet the books and they'd greet him. McDougall's title comes from the famous Parisian bookseller's description of standing before the French Gothic manuscript illuminations of *Les Très Riches Heures du Duc de Berry*. While peering at them, she was able 'to perceive as through a magic emerald the very nature of France: our land and its people dressed in bold colours; gestures of work, as pure as those of Mass; women in flowerlike dresses; fanfares of leisure; living water, branches; desires and loves; beautiful castles in the distance; a comforting sky; our animals near us; our days coloured with hope and finely woven.' Yes, I knew there'd be something there for me. Christopher's poetry was just that, the magic emerald through which one was presented the world anew and in which was brought into play all the colours of the spectrum. Wait a minute: wouldn't *everything* seen through an emerald appear green? I can hear his Shade chuckle at the end of whatever line goes to where he is. Shall we say, rather, that his poetry was a clear prism and that there was no room for greys in his palette? Yes, that'll do.

Simply because one thing leads to another, I go and find Rilke's *Book of Hours* in which one of the poems begins, 'I live my life in widening circles that reach out across the world.' It has been variously translated, sometimes, I suspect, rather clumsily, and my German-speaking friend is not here to advise me on how best to render it for he was one of the very best of translators.

Ich lebe mein Leben in wachsenden Ringen,
die sich über die Dinge ziehn.

It would fit well on a tombstone. Christopher, in his growing immobility, greatly yearned for the world. 'Where would you be, if you could choose?'

I asked him. It was a painful question for him to have to answer, but our talk had already taken us in that direction – there was no going back. 'France, the south of France', he replied. I suspect it was the town where once dwelled Gwen le Gallienne 'the lesbian of Menton' (daughter of poet Richard le Gallienne), and Christopher's charming old landlady Madame Abou with her 'enormously fat dropsical husband', Monsieur Abou, and it was where in 1948, under a Mediterranean sun, he felt as if reborn. But then he writes in one of his poems: 'Now he says there are many places / Not to be gone to. Memory has no desire / To be disappointed.' There was, he complained, nothing one could dig up from the Texan landscape that would be sufficiently ancient enough to feed a hungry imagination. Yet I never knew his mind to starve for long before it latched onto something, which, like a bird tugging at a worm, it could pull from even the most obdurate substance. All it needed was for that same bird to land on the fence, satiated, and he'd capture it live in a poem so you could hear it there. During his last three years he spoke to me of the great difficulty of getting at those things which fed his poetry and yet fed it they did, which is why I hope his spirit will forgive the deliberate irony of my title. The greyness without could do nothing to quell the brightness within. The last two years of his life were spent in an old age residence in Austin, Texas, on Liberty Drive or what we jokingly referred to as Captivity Drive. His move there wasn't a happy experience for him although he allowed that for reasons of health he had little choice in the matter. He did, however, arrange for the whole of his library, which comprised some four thousand volumes, to be transported from his old residence and reassembled in the new, in its original order. My one hope for him, which sadly was not to be realised, was that he would quit this world surrounded by his books. He had his writing desk too, and so he was able to continue, as so few people in his position are able to, within a facsimile of what he was accustomed to. It might have been, in certain respects, a better, brighter place, but it was not of his choice and he was the most particular of men. Besides, it was at too great a distance from the local bar where he loved to chat with the waitresses, extract their stories, and the second-hand bookshop where he'd confabulate with his buddies.

Nobody's Ezekiel: I won't say they were the best poems he ever wrote but they stand among the very best by a man about to leave his ninth decade. There's no calcification between the lines. In them there's the usual Middletonian sense of play, the one difference being that now death presses in from all sides. 'Now captivity among the aged ages me, / painfully the past is now and real', he writes in 'The Typesetter's Visit to Cavafy' and then again in 'My Father's Table':

You draw back to the past
we must fabricate with thought,
and the past responds, for real:
it eats our images up
as often as it is hungry. The more

I know the more I must forget,
and the past will push you on,
as the future pushes you back.

Some of the poems he sent me for comment, others he read to me over the phone. At times, they had me stumped; other times they blazed forth with a light of their own. He could be abstruse at times and I know that my reaction often disappointed him, but it is in the nature of certain poets that their readership must catch up with what they've done. Sometimes the wait is a longish one, though, and for Christopher it had become a matter of some anxiety as to where his place in literature would be. Often, in his darker moments, he would ask why it was that he was ignored by the younger poets, to which I'd always reply, in slightly varying shades, that it was not because those poets were deliberately ignoring him, but because they were almost entirely focussed upon themselves. This has become quite the most selfish of times. Gone are the days when the younger poet looked up to the older, and it's to be wondered if this is the first time in literary history that there's been such a divide. One day I think poets here will wake up to what it was they missed and even now I hear small yelps of lamentation from the direction of poets who, when he was alive, never gave him a moment's credence. Yet Christopher was always one to look to the younger. It was the publication of a poem of mine in this very magazine that inspired him to first write to me in 1992. He was, in this respect, one of the most generous of men, but also he was driven by an enthusiasm that remained undimmed almost right up to the day of his death. He fought back at the inevitable with his poetry and I can't help but think he kept himself alive to see the publication of his final book. It was soon after he received the copies of his last book that he went into decline. The lady who'd earlier captured his affections was now gone from the scene and there was no book in the pipeline. When growing blindness and a hand no longer able to pick up the pen overtook him, there was nothing left for him but to look to his departure. All that he'd set out to do, he'd done.

I suspect he even approached death with curiosity. I never knew a mind more curious than his. A few weeks before he died he discovered in an anthology a poet hitherto unknown to him, Henry King (1592–1669), Bishop of Chichester and it was quite by chance that a day later I located a copy of his poems and sent it to him as quickly as possible. I'll never know whether he had a chance to peruse it although he did thank me for it. Certainly it's hard to believe he was not still composing in his mind when, during the course of our final conversation, only hours before he died, I was able to make out through his strangled voice – for there was some terrible obstruction in his throat – the words, 'This is it.' So terse an utterance it was that the words might well have been the closing sentence of a poem he was working on mentally. As always, he was affectionate in his closing words because he knew they might be his last to me.

Nobody's Ezekiel concludes with a poem that isn't the last he ever wrote but which, in terms of spirit, is. Certainly he knew where in the book it should be positioned and not only because the title of the first poem is 'Flight'. The poem 'Lost Squadron' first came to me over the telephone – it immediately sent a shudder through me. He'd just finished it that morning and I thought immediately of the elderly poet in *Night of the Iguana* who, after a long dry spell, excitedly announces the completion of his new poem, recites it to his granddaughter, just before his cane clatters to the ground and all is over. I remember thinking at the time, almost perversely, may this be his last poem because it's such a good place on which to end.

LOST SQUADRON

Often enough
strapped, sedentary
in the cockpit of my biplane,
I dropped sputtering to earth.

To rise from the waters
Icarus made no effort;
flight like his, for a second or two
seeing the islands, warships,
mountains and city, people crawling...
but life primes itself with legend.

It stared me in the face,
my furrow did. In my wallet,
olives, bread, cheese, and water
cool in the shade,
safely aged.

Allow my distance, daughter,
when I see, from the riverside.
a tribe of cormorants
fly in their formation
as some few friends once did
in their lost squadron.

I asked him to repeat it, which he did and with more oxygen in his voice. I knew he was pleased. Vanity in the best of writers is both true and acceptable. An elderly man in his cockpit, falling to earth, and then suddenly, *whoosh*, a flight of cormorants. This was his mighty gift to poetry: *surprise*. Would it help the reader to know that as a young man, at the end of World War Two, he flew with the RAF? Yes, I think so. The lost squadron is no idle image. Christopher did not, as far as I know, drop any bombs – he was just a bit too late on the scene for that – but he did see some very blatant Nazis lynched. What he implied was that not all was played according to Queensberry rules.

The end when it came stunned me, which isn't to say it was unexpected but because it is very much in the way of things that the expected, when it comes, is always a shock. I seek instances of this in literature. One need look no further than the plays of Sophocles or Shakespeare to realise that a prevailing sense of the inevitable in what drives them gives them their force, and this is why the surrealists with their shock tactics almost always fail to surprise. He always thought I was a bit hard on the latter, but then he was not so riddled with prejudice as I am at times. God, I do so miss our arguments. So it is that the death

of Christopher, at the age of eighty-nine, shocks me. So it is that I want not to hear about 'good innings', a phrase I've always found objectionable. Say, rather, depth increases sorrow.

With Christopher there was always the sense that despite his words to the contrary there'd be one more poem to come or yet another gift from him. Some months ago, he sent me the German-language edition of Zbigniew Herbert's *Pan Cogito*, which the Polish poet inscribed to him when they met in Freiburg in May 1975 and had gone boating together with Herbert's wife, Katarzyna. I imagine a scene such as Renoir might have painted. A few days ago, I heard from his daughter in Paris that she is sending me a book he'd picked up for me some years ago and which he neglected to bring me, maybe because it was too heavy to carry. It always amazed me that when he came to London, sometimes on the way to, sometimes on the way back from, Turkey, he carried nothing more than a small bag just large enough to accommodate a greedy man's lunch. Yet he was always immaculately turned out in cream trousers and in that bag were, in addition to his requirements, a couple of books, his notebooks, and so forth. I never knew a man to travel more lightly, as if he himself walked on air. As he was only in his early eighties when he was last here, I never knew him as the elderly man he'd self-reportedly become. I never quite believed him. Once, when I invited a friend to dinner, he asked me, 'Is he *our* age?' It was true the two decades plus which separated us in years had not done so in spirit, and in truth I think he thrived on the relative youth of others.

I'm waiting for the postman to arrive. The volume on the way to me he picked up in Auvers-sur-Oise in a second-hand bookshop converted from several cars of an old train. What joy that must have given him, moving from carriage to carriage, the walls lined with books, the sheer fun of it. The book is called *The Syriac Chronicle, known as that of Zachariah of Mitylene* (Methuen, 1899). Christopher, in his final years, was fascinated by early Eastern Christianity. Maybe there was a struggle in him over whether to keep it for himself or give it to me and so the book went into limbo. This is as true of me as of all book collectors and so I mean no criticism: I remember him pining for a book of mine which, with no huge regret, I failed to surrender to him, although several other books I did. Such are the breaks when two sets of eager hands reach for the same volume. The quicker triumphs. The book sounds a challenge. Could it be some final message from him, saying, 'Why not grapple with this for a while?' That would be so very much like him.

Seeing Geese Arrive

Christopher Middleton

For Miranda, my daughter in Colorado;
vivid detail in a phone-call from her suggested the poem.

A full moon floated
on air in the twilight,

wrinkled lake below
splashing all of a sudden.

collision, confusion
when a formation of geese

from far off up north
flew in and landed

with such an abnormal
flapping and honking

you started to think
the geese had straddled

two currents, one warmer,
and the cool one beside it,

yes, a river ran though,
prompting alarm from nerve tissue

safe in the weathered goose breast
and sensitive as a testicle.

*

Ages ago they'd say worldwide:
Thus doth spirit crash into matter.

The-ology
On the Definite Article in English Verse
Graham Pechey

Many of my titles in this book have the definite article [...] The reader must not think I am offering him a set of Theophrastean characters. I am not generalizing; 'The Conscript' does not stand for all conscripts but for an imagined individual; any such individual seems to have an absolute quality which the definite article recognizes.

This 'absolute quality' Louis MacNeice claims for the English definite article in his volume *Springboard* (1945) wasn't won early or easily. It is not to be found in all literary contexts; and when modernist poetry gave it its head, it was neither welcomed by all critics nor provided with a basis for understanding by linguists. Linguists tell us that the definite article sprang from a mutation in the paradigm of demonstrative pronouns some eight hundred years ago: a form that had developed in late Anglo-Saxon lost its inflection for gender and number to become the only definite article in Middle English. In so doing it escaped the demonstrative paradigm altogether, setting up a new paradigm in correlation with the independently developing *in*definite article. *The* as a full-fledged definite determiner, then, has been with us for roughly half the life of our language. Grammarians tell us that felicitous uses of the article depend on conditions of 'familiarity' or 'uniqueness' which guarantee its efficacy in pragmatic speech situations. Directions given to a wayfarer – 'Turn left at the church' – would fail to help him if these conditions were not met; they belong therefore, quite legitimately, to the normality and utility of communication.

Poets of course, lyric poets especially, have long enjoyed a limited waiver of these conditions, permitting them to use *the* of something not in the reader's field of vision or knowledge and without prior or anterior (anaphoric or cataphoric) reference in the discourse: think of emblematic topics in old songs such as this one from among the Rawlinson Lyrics MS –

Well was hire bour, / What was hire bour?
    The rede rose and the— The rede rose and the—
Well was hire bour, / What was hire bour?
    The rede rose and the lilie flour

– or of representative types such as 'The ploughman' in Gray's 'Elegy'; or things contingently in the lyricist's immediate environment like 'the still stream' in Keats's 'Nightingale' ode. Those 'absolute' uses of *the* which I've identified with modernism challenge the whole model of semantic perspective upon which both the twentieth-century linguist's happiness conditions and the earlier poet's licensed exemptions are predicated; indeed the exemptions now appear as a new set of verse-specific conditions. Traditionally, all instances of the definite article in a poem must either line up behind a single point of reference or – if there is a shift of alignment – that shift must somehow (in the Russian-Formalist sense) be 'motivated' thematically. This was first forcefully borne in upon me when I read Thomas Dilworth's *Shape and Meaning in the Poetry of David Jones* in which the author of *In Parenthesis* was said to assume 'an intimacy which the reader must work to achieve' and to have imposed upon his work a 'compression that makes [it] difficult of access but lyrically powerful and immediate in tone'. A statistical measure of this assumed intimacy is the incidence in Jones's long prose-poem of 'three times as many definite as indefinite articles' – a mismatch which is surely bound to arise when narrative approximates lyric and a high proportion of the things determined by *the* have not been determined earlier by *a*. Jones was no doubt influenced in this practice by T. S. Eliot, and he was to experiment even more radically with this *the* in priority which is also a *the* of infinite referential variety in later works.

How the Georgian poet and critic George Rostrevor Hamilton would have reacted to Jones we cannot know; Eliot's way with the definite article had already done 'serious damage [...] to the structure of the English language'. The definite article, he writes bluntly in *The Tell-Tale Article: A Critical Study of Modern Poetry* (1949), 'claims our recognition'. W. H. Auden's phrase 'the long aunts' in the volume *Look, Stranger!* (1936) draws from Hamilton the exasperated question: 'How [...] has the article been earned by an image we cannot begin to place?' Unlike the indefinite article – which belongs 'naturally' with the hitherto unmentioned, with statements of the hypothetical or the paradoxical, with something 'which has hardly begun to take form' or which 'runs counter to common experience', the definite article 'relies on a sufficient community of experience to enable the reader to familiarise it in his mind'. For Hamilton, it is as if in modernist verse *the* and *a* have swapped roles, with *the* falling into a sort of limbo between definite and indefinite reference, and amounting almost to an offence against British good manners: the object 'may be so unfamiliar and so doubtfully illuminated by anything in the context [...] it is as though an entire stranger were claiming our acquaintance'. Unpromising as all of this sounds, Hamilton's *The Tell-tale Article* has some interesting things to say about the history of English poetic syntax: parts of his argument can be coaxed obligingly into its own undoing; and we can extract from it a helpful periodisation of the definite article's relative incidence in English verse-writing.

One point in particular deserves our close attention. Hamilton tells us that the writers of the pre-modern and early-modern periods were 'much less concerned' than those of high modernity 'with reflection and description, and dealt more constantly with personal relations, the *he* and the *she*, the *I* and the *thou*, man to God, man to woman'; they were 'given to apostrophe'. Presumably the definite article's prominence in the poetry of the eighteenth and nineteenth centuries meets Hamilton's criterion of the recognizable in so far as the objects to which it is attached are all subsumable under the rubric of Nature, whether defined in deist or pantheist (Popean or Wordsworthian) terms. However that may be, we might connect this development which sees a verse of the preponderant definite article supplanting an earlier verse of intersubjectivity with an arresting concurrence in the history of the language: namely, that the modern *the* was emerging at just the time when the personal pronoun *thee* was moving under the influence of the French *tu-vous* from being the mandatory second-person accusative or dative to being one member of what Roger Brown and Albert Gilman describe in their path-breaking essay 'Pronouns of Power and Solidarity' (1960) as the 'power semantic'. One then gave *thee* only to social equals and subordinates, whilst the plural *you* was given to one's betters. God, however, was still addressed as *thee* – partly no doubt because it had always been thus in the Latin of the liturgy; partly because the power semantic was felt to belong to worldly hierarchies in which deity had no part; but more deeply still perhaps because this coincidence enacted the Christian paradox of a God who empties Himself to become one of us. Now in mediaeval manuscripts the definite article and the second-person dative-accusative regularly appear as homographs, suggesting that they were homophones in speech. Materiality and meaning in language being inextricably bound up, homonymy prompting synonymy in the spontaneous folk etymology of speakers, could it be that emerging *the* caught from mutating *thee* something at least of that pronoun's evocative coextension of the intimate and the infinite?

Bizarre as my speculation might sound in a disenchanted post-Cartesian context, it becomes less so when we remember that for the denizens of pre-modern England the world was a *plenum* replete with animacy and addressability in all its elements. But there is a further and fascinating connection between animacy and the definite article in the history of a language much older than English: in his commonplace book *A Certain World* (1971), Auden quotes a passage from Bruno Snell's *The Discovery of the Mind* (1982 [1953]) in which Snell not only attributes the capacity of Greek philosophy to 'formulate the universal as a particular' to the language's possession of the definite article but also claims that behind such abstract nouns as Plato's 'the Good' are mythical names such as Homer's 'the Frightener':

Many words which were later regarded as abstracts began their career as mythical names. In Homer [...] fear appears as a demon, as the Frightener, the *Phobos.* The extent to which these words were understood as names, even after the mythic connotation had long worn off, is evident from the use of the article [...] If the definite article had not permitted the framing of these 'abstractions' as we call them, it would have been impossible to develop an abstract concept from an adjective or a verb, or to formulate the universal as a particular [...] Cicero has to fall back upon circumlocutions [... in translating Plato] *to agathon* (the good) is: *id quod (re vera) bonum est.*

Even as they inaugurate a new world purged of the personal, then, the names of concepts are haunted by the ghosts of the demon or deity that the article had once denoted.

Now Homer having been little more than hearsay in the Middle Ages, the Greek article was unlikely to have provided a learned model for the rising English definite. The actual history is more complex: both Greek and Hebrew having boasted the definite article, it might be argued that Christianity's invention of itself as a discourse to rival Greek philosophy was made possible by the work of the Greek definite in translating and re-accenting its Hebrew counterpart. Ironically, though, it was article-free Latin which carried the faith from its near-Eastern source to territories where local vernaculars would at length invent their own definite articles. Middle English, with its flexible and single definite, was the first in the field to realise the possibility thus opened up of the article's restoration to the sacred text. *In principio erat verbum* from the gospel of John becomes 'In the bigynnyng was the word'; Jesus's *sub ficu* becomes 'vndur the fige tree'; and Nathanael's *Filius Dei* becomes 'the sone of God'. *The* is the agent here of a remarkable kenotic exchange: Jesus uses that word to establish a temporal uniqueness; Nathanael uses it in turn to acknowledge the eternal uniqueness of the god-man speaking to him. This grammatical common denominator of heaven and earth then invigorates with the ambivalence shown in this biblical example a whole range of genres in verse and prose. *The* is thereby launched as the place in English where immanent and transcendent, narrative and the numinous, humble and elevated meet. It is this extraordinary operator of simultaneous ascent and descent that is bequeathed to the whole English verse tradition then emerging.

Digging back into the prehistory of the article in this way helps us to overcome the blindness of a Hamilton when it comes to evaluating the work of Eliot and Auden. That modernist verse restores the dynamic of its pre-modern forebear under new conditions can be most graphically illustrated by means of an analogy from the visual arts. Marshall McLuhan distinguishes between 'picturesque' – Tennyson is his prime example – and 'symbolist' poetry:

The picturesque artists saw the wider range of experience that could be managed by discontinuity and planned irregularity, but they kept to the picture-like single perspective. The interior landscape, however, moves naturally towards the principle of multiple perspectives as in the first two lines of *The Waste Land* where [...] Chaucer, Sir James Frazer and Jessie Weston are simultaneously present. This is 'cubist perspective' which renders, at once, a diversity of views with the spectator always in the centre of the picture, whereas in picturesque art the spectator is always outside ('Tennyson and Picturesque Poetry', 1951).

Applying this to our topic, we might say that high-modern *the* presupposes the linear and external perspective of McLuhan's picturesque; the modernist *the* plunges us into the planar multiplicity of 'cubist perspective'. Boris Uspensky's remarks on the 'inverse perspective' of pre-modern painting in *A Poetics of Composition* (1973) complement those of McLuhan:

In painting, and in the other visual arts, point of view is primarily connected with perspective. Linear perspective, a normative concept in European painting since the Renaissance, assumes a single static point of view, a single static position from which the object is viewed [...] A plurality of viewpoints is characteristic of mediaeval art, particularly in the complex phenomenon called inverse perspective.

Uspensky enables us not only to find a correlative for the work of *the* in pre-modern verbal contexts, but also prompts the realization that that article's behaviour in modernist verse constitutes a return to the old 'plurality of viewpoints'. However reduced its role had been in the verse of the high-modern period, when the universal particulars it characteristically generated were of notably modest metaphysical reach, in late modernity it has revived something at least of its earlier scope and power. It has even acquired the skill of scoring high in effect by selectively absenting itself from the textual scene in places where we'd expect to find it. MacNeice plays with this elision notably well – think of 'world' in his poem 'Snow' – and Auden in turn is notable for what MacNeice calls in his *Selected Literary Criticism* (1987) a style of 'beautiful telegraphese'. Let us look first at Eliot.

Transgressive use of the definite article starts in *The Waste Land* (1922) with the title, which is less a guide to some empirical location unifying all of its detail than a licence for *nova* to offer themselves as *data* throughout the poem. Shifts of perspective triggered by phrases like 'the dead land', 'the Starnbergersee', 'the hyacinth garden' and 'the Hanged Man' are thrust upon us with zero motivation in narrative or expository terms. If in the legendary source from which Eliot extracts the waste-land motif – namely, the Grail story – that very phrase 'the (Holy) Grail' is an instance of the pre-modern definite at work, evoking as it does the uniqueness of a divine Absolute, there is for Eliot no simple return to this textual correlative of the icon except circuitously, by the way of multiple perspectives undoing the presupposition of a fixed earthly standpoint. The voice in 'The Hollow Men' (1925) which cannot get further in the doxology of the Lord's Prayer than its opening four words ('For thine is the') foregrounds *the* by

leaving it in textual mid-air, thereby generating a proposition which could launch a treatise on the Divine Nature or on the definite article or both together. In the lines 'The vanished power of the usual reign' and 'The infirm glory of the positive hour' from *Ash-Wednesday* I (1930), those two noun phrases are so far from being illuminated by the adjectival phrases qualifying them that they actually plunge us deeper into perplexity. That is, until we hear distantly echoed in their principal nouns the three attributes missing from the 'Hollow Men' speaker's truncated doxology – *power, reign* and *glory* being applied ironically not to the Godhead but to human agency, and specifically to an already 'vanished' and 'infirm' fantasy of control on the would-be penitent's part.

In 'Who walked between the violet and the violet' from *Ash-Wednesday* III, the oddity of that adverbial phrase is resolved when *violet* is grasped alternately as flower and colour, as contingent object or as something approximating a Platonic Idea. We might therefore read the line as a poetic realization of something Eliot had earlier written as a student in his *Knowledge and Experience in the Philosohy of F.H. Bradley* (1964): 'It was known, I should suppose, by Plato that universals and particulars cannot be in any meaningful sense related, inasmuch as they are not separate existences'. The line 'The woodthrush singing through the fog' from *Marina* (1930) draws us in as co-listeners as any such set of words in a Romantic lyric would, only then to recur as 'the woodsong fog', a nonce-compound in which the elements of the first phrase are so condensed as to portend a non-relational 'felt whole' of Bradleian 'immediate experience' in which the bird and the ground from which its song emerges are indistinguishable. It is as if the original phrase has too much grammar for its own good and must be reconfigured as a once-off neologism if it is to be signed into the unanalysable singularity of 'an all-inclusive experience outside of which nothing shall fall'. By the end, with 'woodthrush calling through the fog / My daughter', speaker and bird have merged. Mutating *the* has been the agent of an epiphany for the speaker, who has 'resigned [his] life' for the new life promised by his imminently reappearing daughter.

Auden's early pastiche of an Anglo-Saxon elegy in *Poems* (1933) is as free of *the* as any of its Old English models:

Doom is dark and deeper than any sea-dingle.
Upon what man it fall
In spring, day-wishing flowers appearing,
Avalanche sliding, white snow from rock-face,
That he should leave his house [...]
[...] lonely on fell as chat,
By pot-holed becks
A bird stone-haunting, an unquiet bird.

The poem's peculiar grammar enacts for us the status of its wandering protagonist as a cipher condemned to sheer seriality of experience in an unsignified, unsanctified world. 'On this Island' from *Look, Stranger!* (1936) for its part draws us in with the well-behaved definites of the high-modern insular tradition; subtly syncopates its music in the second stanza; and then surprises us in the last by forsaking altogether the stabilities of the present and clearly visible for the far-off and not-yet:

Look, stranger, at this island now
The leaping light for your delight discovers,
Stand stable here
And silent be,
That through the channels of the ear
May wander like a river
The swaying sound of the sea.

Here at the small field's ending pause
Where the chalk wall falls to the foam and its tall ledges
Oppose the pluck
And knock of the tide,
And the shingle scrambles after the suck-
-ing surf, and the gull lodges
A moment on its sheer side.

Far off like floating seeds the ships
Diverge on urgent voluntary errands,
And the full view
Indeed may enter
And move in memory as now these clouds do,
That pass the harbour mirror
And all the summer through the water saunter.

'Diverge on urgent voluntary errands' ominously shifts the poem's core register to the Latinate lexis of news reports, and 'the full view' teases the listening 'stranger' with the threat that this aesthetic consummation transcending what can be seen here and now will be less a completion of the natural beauty of the shore-line than its menacing man-made opposite, fraught with a wider history. In 'Spain 1937' from *Another Time* – a poem *one in five* of whose words is the definite article – this view was to be resolved into an abstraction, 'the struggle':

Yesterday the theological feuds in the taverns
    And the miraculous cure at the fountain;
Yesterday the Sabbath of Witches. But today the struggle.

Soon that brutally frontal political absolute was to meet its match in a neo-Metaphysical lyric from the same volume which notably raises the article's game and is almost a divine comedy in miniature:

Warm are the still and lucky miles,
White shores of longing stretch away,
A light of recognition fills
   The whole great day, and bright
The tiny world of lovers' arms.

Silence invades the breathing wood
Where drowsy limbs a treasure keep,
Now greenly falls the learned shade
   Across the sleeping brows
And stirs their secret to a smile.

Restored! Returned! The lost are borne
On seas of shipwreck home at last:
See! In a fire of praising burns

The dry dumb past, and we
Our life-day long shall part no more.

Love as at once *eros* and *agape* is obliquely hinted in a music of subtle internal rhymes and grammat-ically 'rhyming' phrases as the 'the dry dumb past' is purgatorially consumed in 'the fire of praising'.

In Jones's later writing – much admired by Auden – the indefinite article is almost nowhere to be found, and instead of the *a/the* logic of tradi-tional lyric or narrative, a logic of *the*/zero-article or *the*/all predominates, as in this example from 'The Tutelar of the Place' (1974):

Gathering all things in, twining each bruised stem to the swaying trellis of the dance, the dance about the sawn lode-stake on the hill where the hidden stillness is at the core of struggle, the dance around the green lode-tree on far fair-height where the secret guerdons hang and the bright prizes nod, where sits the queen *im Rosenhage* eat-ing the honey-cake, where the king sits, counting-out his man-geld, rhyming the audits of all the world-holdings.

That word 'Gathering' launches a dance of right-branching relative clauses in which May-pole and rood-tree coincide and all things are recon-ciled around the still point of the Absolute. Here, we feel, is where *the* primally belongs, in or near 'the hidden stillness', subserving the exceptionless, absolved from all conditions, wedding the near to the far. The distinction between foreground and background is every bit as undecidable in Jones's painting. In his 'Annunciation', for example, the plane which shows the Blessed Virgin Mary and the archangel Gabriel shows also – without reces-sion – birds and flowers, of which Rowan Williams remarks in *Grace and Necessity* (2005) (watch the definite articles at work in his prose): 'they are the mobile life of an actual landscape that is being 're-lit' by the non-local but utterly concrete presence of the coming of the Word of God.'

When Auden, in 'Adam as a Welshman' (1963), claims that proper nouns are 'the most conspic-uous features' of Jones's verse, it is hard to resist the conclusion that the honorary proper nouns generated by the definite article are potential micro-poems, and that achieved poems are (con-versely) definite articles writ large. It comes as no surprise that in Jones this rule of the proper noun goes along with a predilection to encyclopaedic particularities of time and place: something he shares with James Joyce – Joyce, inspirational for both Eliot and Jones, and the author of a novel which *ends* with the definite article.

This audacity was some time preparing. Earlier modernist fiction – for example, in the opening sentences of Henry James's *What Maisie Knew* (1897) – uses the unidentified definites of cata-phoric reference in a feint of the reader's partial inwardness with the plot business just beginning:

The litigation had seemed interminable and had in fact been complicated; but by the decision on the appeal the judgement of the divorce-court was confirmed as to the assignment of the child. The father, who, though bespattered from head to foot, had made good his case, was, in pursuance of this triumph, appointed to keep her [...]

Joyce is the next stage. Whilst Stephen's 'Ineluctable modality of the visible' from *Ulysses* (1922) breaks new ground beyond James, it enjoys residual realistic motivation in the new convention of so-called 'interior monologue'. According to Joseph Frank, Joyce 'assumes – what is obviously not true – that his readers are Dubliners, intimately acquainted with Dublin life and the personal history of his characters': where cataphoric reference is no longer merely a local device (paradoxically engaging and estranging) but a universal principle of structuring, pattern is elevated over narrative, and – that pattern being forever out of reach – the reader is given a profound sense of his or her finitude; all objects of allusion then have about them an immemorial familiarity for *someone else* which makes them so many contextual absolutes. The last sentence of *Finnegans Wake* (1939) is a parody of the *a*/*the* logic of linear narrative and, in its invitation to us to step into the 'riverrun' and begin again, reference 'forward' and reference 'backward' cease to make any directional sense:

Finn, again! Take. Bussoftlhee, mememormee! Till thousendsthee. Lps. The keys to. Given! A way a lone a last a loved a long the

Modernist verse and modernist fiction converge, then, in their deployment of absolute *the* or its analogues; and there is a beneficent complementarity between the respectively carnivalesque and incarnational aesthetics towards which this discovery

(or recovery) inflects them. We have arrived at a point where the pun in my title might not after all be arbitrary: theology is perhaps inscribed in the language, and the definite article utterly loosed from its constraints promises an oblique theophany, even if that vision is vouchsafed only to a reader happy to suspend disbelief. The real hero of the Grail story is perhaps not the Quester so much as the article which renders the high uniqueness of its object across several European vernaculars, and in which all of the writers I've discussed have some investment. Four of them are Catholics of one or other stripe – Anglo- or Roman or lapsed – and they display symbolic imaginations to match. The single greatest pioneer of the modern European imagination was the poet who did more than any other to purify a tribal dialect of Latin; a poet whose importance for Eliot (among other modernist writers) could scarcely be exaggerated; and of whose work of elaborating paradox as intricate poetic action Charles Williams has written in *The Figure of Beatrice* (1943):

It was, however high the phrases, the common thing from which Dante always started, as it was certainly the greatest and most common to which he came. His images were the natural inevitable images – the girl in the street, the people he knew, the language he learned as a child. In them the great diagrams were perceived; from them the great myths open; by them he understands the final end.

The last century saw the great myths being *re*-opened in its most innovative writing, with a very small part of speech playing no small part in that revival.

Peak District

Vidyan Ravinthiran

'The young lambs bound / As to the tabour's sound'.
They toss and toss: it is as if it were the earth that flung them, not themselves.
It is the pitch of graceful agility when we think that.

– Gerard Manley Hopkins

The lambs wear fuchsia digits,
wisps of torn cloud

hang from the bossy
roots of hugging beeches
planted close to meld into one bole;

also the wire

whose barbs rust first, drop out and leave
inches of clear air

where harm should be . . .

~

Why are we here? To flee
our inboxes
stuffed with silence

or rejections; to peer,
half-cut, down a blue road,
phone aloft, hunting for pockets of signal . . .

After killing the bottle,
it nevertheless became possible
to say and do wonderful things to each other.

~

So here I am,
squeezed by the arm

by you
as the cavern guide quips, off-colour

about the light and dark Peaks
and some biddie glares

in a one-street village
while we scoff wraps on her stone bench.

~

Still, onward
you drive us, fast and sure around the lake
the clouds turn mauve

before they swing apart
and the sun bangs off the water
and we race

past, squinting into the glitter
like so many camera flashes going off
in a stadium crowd.

~

Reversing onto beige gravel,
we climb down and try and fail
to skim some stones. Above us, in the blue air,

the verge-lopped torsos of the brown
family, stood by their hired van;
the father and the uncle pore over,

brows furrowed, map and guidebook.
Glancing up, they beat me to the question:
What are you looking at?

~

It smashed itself, quite spontaneously.
The mid-pane of our patio door. While we were out.

Leaving us, that evening – our second
candlelit dinner, stilted, emulous – without,

bouncing on their twilit hill,
the distraction of the adorable lambs.

Watching, instead, how *the many-colour'd glass*
cracked and crazed and gave back

our restive fire. A spider-web of lava
emerged of green grass and blue mountains.

Boy with a Coney
Laura Kilbride

for Ian Patterson

Hearing of molten rock which fell to mountains,
meeting with three-faced statues on the beaches,
returning suddenly to the fact of marble
on sand dunes where the wind whips round my ankles,
we honour sculptors of these sacred places
whose sculpture marks the limits of our honour.

Once the gods were worthy of our honour
keeping to hidden pathways in the mountains
they spoke through fields of fire in certain places
and met with mortals. On these blackened beaches
the goddess held Achilles by the ankles
and he grew god and knew it, strong as marble.

Who poets sing of, sculptors wrest in marble –
the god's own likeness people likewise honour
and tie their sacred garlands round his ankles.
Yet even these strong gods into the mountains
fled when men with strange nets on their beaches
landed and raised to earth their temple places.

And they erected churches in their places
from broken *stelae*, culled from purest marble.
The people gathered on their sunburnt beaches
and came to pay the *pantocrator* honour –
though some remembered old gods in the mountains
and wept to tie their garlands round his ankles.

And some believed the nails had pierced his ankles
and not his hands or feet. In certain places
where sea and sky are met and in the mountains
the people came again to trust in marble
and golden garlands – though there are some who honour
the god who walked among them on the beaches

and still he walks. Now, far from these beaches,
a sculptor carves a boy with powerful ankles
in animal lines. The people come to honour
the blood-red stone, and in these white washed places
the live stone falls again through art to marble –
the gods shall not return now from the mountains.

Can we call this honour? Venerating marble,
washed up on the beaches, or fallen in the mountains
wading in these places, the wind around our ankles.

Lipari, Lent 2015
Originally published in *The Junket*

Aspermatic Days and Nights (II)
Samuel Beckett and an Anti-Genealogy of Contemporary Irish Poetry
David Wheatley

Within a decade Beckett would be fighting typhoid in post-war Normandy, working for the Red Cross, as recorded in his radio talk 'Capital of the Ruins'. One poem from this period that inhabits a somewhat orphaned state within the canon is 'Antipepsis', unpublished in Beckett's lifetime and unlike any of the poems in French or English written during this period. Its rollicking octosyllabics place it in the tradition of Swift but also, in more recent times, that of Joyce's 'Gas from a Burner' and 'The Holy Office'. Nevertheless, it is highly unusual to find Beckett employing 'a form of terminal consonance no longer permitted', as Pound sarcastically called rhyme when he returned to it for his satirical poem of 1915, 'L'Homme Moyen Sensuel':

And the number was uneven
In the green of holy Stephen
Where before the ass the cart
Was harnessed for a foreign part.
In this should not be seen the sign
Of hasard, no, but of design,
For of the two, by common consent,
The cart was the more intelligent.
Whose exceptionally pia
Mater hatched this grand idea
Is not known. He or she,
Smiling, unmolested, free,
By this one act the mind become
A providential vacuum,
Continues still to run amok.
To eat, drink, piss, shit, fart and fuck,
Assuming that the fucking season
Did not expire with that of reason.
Now through the city spreads apace
The cry: A thought has taken place!
A human thought! Ochone! Ochone!
Purissima Virgo! We're undone!
Bitched, buggered and bewilderèd!
Bring forth your dead! Bring forth your dead!

Beckett liked the Gaelic imprecation 'ochone' enough to use it again in an uncollected *mirliton-nade* thirty years later ('ochone ochone / dead and not gone'). The distress of the natives signals their opposition to the rule of 'reason', but Beckett's adherence to the line of Anglo-Irish rationalism turns out to be less than full-blooded. Intertextual evidence for this turns up two lines later with his use of the word 'bitched', spoken by the hapless Dubliners at the prospect of a nascent thought, but repeated by Hamm in *Endgame* when he finds a flea in his trousers which he fears will go on to repopulate the earth. The occasion of outrage differs, but in each case it is the cry of pain in the face of generation that finds most eloquent voice, certainly more so than the aloof voice of 'reason' in 'Antipepsis'. The 'providential vacuum' in which the Irish mind runs riot overlaps with the

'no-man's-land, Hellespont or vacuum' of artistic production in 'Recent Irish Poetry', but here again condemnation (of the first) and advocacy (of the second) overlap suggestively. The closing instruction to 'Bring forth your dead' smacks of Daniel Defoe's *A Journal of the Plague Year* (Defoe being a frequent reference point for Beckett), but bringing forth his dead, or undead in the case of Belacqua, was an activity the young Beckett found all too attractive. The relationship between Beckett and that arch satirist of Free State Catholic Ireland, Austin Clarke, has been much analysed: despite their shared recoil from clerical hegemony, the version of Clarke depicted as Austin Ticklepenny in *Murphy* has been broken by Catholic Ireland, become its prisoner and plaything. Yet the satirist of 'Antipepsis' too finds himself, paradoxically, embracing his condition of imprisonment – escaping only by the ultimate trapdoor. We are back to the shadowless vampire satire of 'Echo's Bones', a literally underground perspective on Catholic Ireland.

A literal rather than knowing sterility overtakes Beckett's poetry in the post-war period, as he takes a leave of absence from verse composition that lasts over two decades, excepting poems written for works in other forms such as the 'Song' from *Words and Music*. Beckett took a hard line on the mixing of genres where adaptations of his work were concerned, but late Beckett is also characterised by a closing of the gap between genres – the imperative verbs of the short prose texts of the sixties, as though reeling off stage directions; the incorporation of texts and self-conscious textuality into the plays, as in *Ohio Impromptu*. When Beckett does return to poetry, it follows this trend. Much has changed from the boisterous lyrics of *Echo's Bones*. If we go in search of 'aspermatic' poems from these years, what we find are poems that, often enough, appear to have dispensed with the body altogether. Where previously the female body was an object of grotesque derision or cowed adoration, here it has moved into the realm of shades familiar from plays such as *Footfalls*, *That Time* or the Yeats-referencing *... but the clouds*. Many of the exquisite short poems of the *mirlitonnades* conduct their business without any use for personal pronouns; in his *Cambridge Introduction to Modern Irish Poetry* Justin Quinn ticks me off for rendering the opening poem of that sequence, '*en face / le pire / jusqu'à ce / qu'il fasse rire*' as 'Facing / the worst / laugh / till you burst', introducing a 'you' 'whereas the original has just a statement of general, detached necessity.

Early Beckett had his 'wombtomb' and the late poems have their own shady equivalent. The French poem '*hors crâne seul dedans*' mentions 'Bocca dans la glace'. This is Bocca degli Abbati, the Ghibelline traitor enclosed in ice in *Inferno* XXXII, a tomb from which (against his will, and only after some violence from Dante) the dead man's story is delivered for our consumption. Interiority is the norm in the early poems, but the relationship of inside and outside has become complex in late Beckett. Bocca's skull is '*pris dans le dehors*', stuck in the outside, but when we hear a noise from without in the poem's not-quite-translation, 'Something There', it is tracked by a skull which is itself a 'whole globe', suggesting any sounds may have been inside, not outside the head (cf. the fourth *mirlitonnade*, in which an ill-seen vision of 'something there' is likewise dismissed: '*la tête le calma disant /ce ne fut que dans ta tête*'). While the practicality of pulling a ghost's hair, as Dante does to Bocca, has always been lost on me, we have now entered a realm beyond the merely physical, or shadowed at all times by the ghostly visitants. For the critic concerned to trace these poems' descent from the Irish tradition, the pickings might appear slim; and in the absence of connecting gestures to a recognisable tradition, there is always the temptation to simply invent them. Reading Derek Mahon's translation of the *mirlitonnade* beginning '*plus loin un autre commémore*' Stephen Watt wonders why Mahon has changed the poem's death date on the gravestone from 1932 to 1922, before deciding it can only be for reasons of the Irish Civil War, nothing significant having occurred in 1932.

No less than Beckett's poetry itself, its afterlife has a tale to tell of the possibilities of the Irish modernist poem. Thomas Kinsella includes Beckett in his *New Oxford Book of Irish Verse* and is not without a Beckettian dimension of his own, as illuminated principally by Derval Tubridy, but his placing of Beckett within the Irish tradition points to persistent problems of categorisation. In *The Dual Tradition* Kinsella tells us that, coming from his 'upper middle class' background, Beckett 'uprooted himself', taking 'very little' with him as he went. Having surprisingly described the fifteen-line 'what would I do without this world' as a 'standard Romantic sonnet', Kinsella seeks in vain for its national coordinates: 'the particulars don't matter; nor the language of non-communication [...] or anything in the nature of a tradition. An entire dimension is missing.' This was twenty years ago, and goes against the more recent orthodoxy of the Irish Beckett – Irish even in his resistance to Irishness – but Kinsella's rootless, orphaned Beckett is not the poet I have been describing. 'Outside of here it's death', Hamm intones in *Endgame*, and having waved Beckett off into the blue yonder of the world beyond Ireland, Kinsella returns to bewailing the persistence back at home of 'obsolete attitudes [...] where the old colonial element is strong'. Beckett steps aside from the British-Irish opposition, but in doing so ends up precisely nowhere. Nowheres *are* congenial locations for Beckett, but where this discovery might be a starting point for a whole new map of Irish poetry, for Kinsella it brings the discussion to a close.

No genealogy of Irish poetry since Kinsella can expect to bypass Seamus Heaney, but attempts to locate a Beckett gene in Heaney's writing quickly run into problems. Heaney is not, to be blunt, an especially Beckettian writer. When he invokes him in his Nobel lecture, it is in the context of art and atrocity. Just as we admire Paul Celan's 'stricken destiny as Holocaust survivor' so too we salute 'Beckett's demure heroism as a member of the French resistance'. Without Heaney quoting Adorno's maxim on art after Auschwitz, Beckett becomes a token of scruple before the gaudiness of art, and one whose example Heaney emulated through the dark years of the Troubles, when he remained 'bowed to the desk like some monk bowed over his prie-dieu', or '*pressé contre ma vieille planche vérolée du noir*' as Beckett puts it in his elegy for his friend Arthur Darley, '*Mort de A. D.*' This being a Nobel lecture, there is an expectation of an evolutionary narrative, from honoured forebears to present-day laureate. Heaney delivers on this with an account of turning away from this stony vision, and 'mak[ing] space in my reckoning and imagining for the marvellous as well as for the murderous', the implication being that the 'marvellous' lay beyond Beckett's range. The only other reference to Beckett in Heaney's critical prose is also an act of deflection from negativity. It occurs in his reading of Philip Larkin's 'Aubade', 'Joy or Night?', an attack on the English poet for failing to deliver the ballooning uplift Heaney considers intrinsic to the work of art. He draws a distinction between Larkin and Beckett: 'Beckett is a very clear example of a writer who is Larkin's equal in not flinching from the ultimate bleakness of things, but who then goes away to do something positive with the bleakness.' Beckett's pessimism is 'apparent' rather than authentic, a staging post in the artistic process, overcome by his 'transformation' of unpromising material. No amount of willed uplift can disguise the poverty, as a critical spectacle, of Beckett 'doing something positive' with the experiences that produced *Endgame*. We must look elsewhere for Beckett's bastard poetic progeny.

In differentiating Beckett from Heaney we are returned to problems of form and problems *with* form. Paul Muldoon has engaged more closely with Beckett than Heaney (Mary Farl Powers' scholarly work on Beckett forms a point of connection in 'Yarrow', and a sequence in *Maggot* is titled 'Lines on the Centenary of the Birth of Samuel Beckett'), but Muldoon's interactions with Beckett are subject to much the same qualification that obtains with Stephen Watt's chosen examples in his *Beckett and Contemporary Irish Writing* – they are rarely with Beckett the poet. Reviewing Beckett's *Collected Poems*, Muldoon spells out his problems with Beckett's poetry: 'Beckett has almost no sense of how a line functions in verse making. To describe his line breaks as arbitrary would be a kindness.' Another difficulty, he continues, is the influence of Beckett's 'contemporaries in Irish modernism, notably Thomas MacGreevy'. In Beckett's defence the example Muldoon proceeds to give is 'For Future Reference', one of the most purely shapeless examples of Beckett's juvenilia, but the sharp edge of disagreement is worth dwelling on. Making allowances for the polemical dimension to 'Recent Irish Poetry' and the vagaries of Beckett's career that kept him from his poetry for whole decades, what remains in the bloodstream of Irish poetry today of the modernist poetics preached by Beckett?

As my last two examples suggest, Northern Ireland and the poetic avant-garde have not enjoyed an easy relationship in recent times, possibly for reasons to do with Louis MacNeice and his role in the tussle for the Yeatsian mantle in the 1930s. While I have argued against the continuities between Beckett and Seamus Heaney, a Northern Irish poet with a more convincing case for upholding the Beckett line is Ciaran Carson. Carson is unusual among contemporary Irish poets in having changed his style radically in mid-career, arguably not once but twice. After his début collection, *The New Estate and Other Poems* in 1976, Carson waited over a decade before publishing *Belfast Confetti* and *The Irish for No*, celebrated for their shaggy-dog stories and Belfast psychogeography; but in 2003 he changed his style again with *Breaking News*, a volume that combines poetic minimalism and use of found material. Four further volumes in the same style have followed: *On the Night Watch*, *Until Before After*, *In the Light Of*, and *From Elsewhere* – volumes closer in style to the Language poetry of Rae Armantrout and Lyn Hejinian than to most of the poetry now being written in Ireland. In *From Elsewhere* Carson harnesses the to-and-fro of translation in a richly Babelian style. The use of translation as a governing metaphor is highly Beckettian, and though the second language in question is French, Carson has performed similar experiments with the Irish language too (something of a blind spot for Beckett). His interactions with second and third languages undermine the primacy of the 'home' language to leave us with what we might call – on the model of MacDiarmid's 'synthetic Scots' – synthetic rather than organic English, an impeccably denatured and estranged lingua franca.

My argument has come up against paradoxes of sterility and generation at every turn, and the expectation that Beckett should produce organic poetic issue may represent a misprision or even betrayal. Histories of the avant-garde are full of gaps, such as the decade-long silences endured by the thirties Irish modernists or the Objectivists; litanies of the lost (the vanishing acts of Rosemary Tonks and Lynette Roberts); fall narratives (the routing of Eric Mottram from the Poetry Society in the 1970s); and outright conspiracy theories (no examples required). Is there not a case for defending the gapped record of avant-garde poetics as one of its defining conditions? I have limited myself thus far to poets who have postdated Beckett, but were we constructing a genealogy of Irish poetic radicalism the name James Clarence Mangan would be sure to feature; yet the first essay-collection devoted to that poet appeared in 2014, one hundred and sixty-five years after his death. Radical Irish poetics, if such a thing even exists, follows no academic clock or generational deadlines. Throughout his work, Beckett considered gaps and silences intrinsic to his technique: writing to Axel Kaun, he dreams of a literature 'dissolved [...] torn by enormous pauses'; and the narrator of *Dream of Fair to Middling Women* announces that 'The experience of my reader shall be between the phrases, in the silence, communicated by the intervals, not the terms, of the statement'. The insistence on what 'Recent Irish Poetry' calls the 'rupture of the lines of communication' is firstly a rejection of formal plenitude in favour of unpunctuated free verse of a kind that intrigued and alarmed Yeats in equal part when he watched Ezra Pound wrench the 1890s lyric into the age of Imagism and its Vorticist

offspring. This rejection is not one that has persisted in the work of apparently more Beckettian poets than Heaney, such as Derek Mahon and Harry Clifton, who are concerned with themes of exile and cosmopolitanism. In his essays on Beckett's poetry, Mahon reflects a tension between Beckett's centrifugal tendencies and a desire to smooth these back over in more settled lyric forms. One essay locates Beckett in the 'metaphysical disjunction between "subject" and "object"', working from 'a different set of premises' from that of the 'mainstream of English poetry'; another hails his 'existential lyric', stressing the mellifluousness with which Beckett seasons his apocalyptic visions.

The question of mellifluousness allows us to enter a comparison from critical theory on modern music, that art form that has so often furnished Beckett with creative exemplars. In his *Philosophy of Modern Music* Adorno compares Schoenberg and Stravinsky, idolizing the first as much as he execrates the second. For Adorno, Stravinsky's embrace of neo-classicism is a betrayal of the avant-garde, not that he considered Stravinsky's earlier work avant-garde either. His later compositions, Adorno writes, 'sound as though they were dangling on strings', employing 'consonances which are twisted in their very joints'. The neo-classical proposes a return to formal resolution where, the hardline modernist insists, no resolution is possible: it is not organic form but a kitsch substitute. It would be easy to paint Mahon and Clifton's poems of exile and character sketches of the great modernists as exercises in heritage modernism, with their use of Pound, Brecht and Camus as outsider artists rather than the contemporary Tom Raworth or J. H. Prynne. Are we ready for a poetic portrait of Beckett in *ottava rima*, charting the composition of *Lessness* and *Ping*? Conversely, the avant-garde risks becomes an enemy of promise in its own right when it hardens into dogma. One of the composers doing most to create a new musical language at the time of Adorno's *Philosophy of Modern Music* was Ligeti, whose orchestral pieces of the 1960s show a strong affinity with Beckett's prose works from this period, but when he embraced a tonal style with his *Trio for Violin, Horn and Piano* in 1982 he provoked fury from former comrades in arms. (Beckett's audience, by contrast, has been singularly lacking in anyone prepared to shout 'Judas!') Defending Ligeti from accusations of betrayal, Gavin Thomas has written: 'Anyone can write a C major triad, but to reimagine that chord and reinvent its context whilst retaining one's own highly idiosyncratic personality is a rare and special achievement.' This seems to me a wise approach for reconciling the competing claims of experimental and formal traditions, or for questioning their mutual hostility as a *donnée* in any given debate. It also provides a way into late Beckett poems such as 'Roundelay', 'thither' and 'one dead of night' – texts as bleached and defamiliarised as *Ping* yet as warm and approachable, in their way, as late Ligeti piano *études*.

To return to our roll-call of modern Irish poets: much like Seamus Heaney, Eavan Boland is not an especially Beckettian poet, but when she titles a volume of essays *A Journey with Two Maps* she signals the potential we unlock when we bifurcate the usual straight roads of Irish literary history.

The rather more Beckettian Catherine Walsh demonstrates this in the first poem of her 2005 collection *City West* when she unfurls two versions of the same sentence down the page in the style we associate with Open Field or Projectivist poetics:

```
there is
        a           in a
    clearer             clearer
light
                    light


    stark               stark
boles           boles
    bark                bark
lifting         lifting


                    layer
layer
   of           experience
    defence
      the curved         curving


                    circumference
circumference
                    V's
of V's
```

From the look of those final V's two roads have diverged here, and sorry we might be that we cannot travel both, to paraphrase Robert Frost. Yet the differences between them appear minimal enough, with the forking V's bending into the accommodating form of a shared 'circumference'. Perhaps this is Walsh's comment on the tendency of divergent paths to end up in the same place, in the eternally recurring boom-to-bust cycle of modern Irish life described in her collection. Beckett too is fond of mapping actual journeys onto literary form, as in the late text (one is tempted to say prose poem) 'The Way', whose separate ways 'were one-way', forming a circuit of the infinity symbol reproduced half-way through the text.

While the infinity symbol allows for journeys without end, it does so within a closed circuit 'Forth and back across a barren same winding one-way way', as Beckett writes. Yet to think a limit is also to think beyond this limit, as Beckett's comedy of self-overcoming reductivism displays time and again. In frisking his successors for signs of their Beckettian sympathies, I have directed sceptical remarks in the direction of Kinsella, Heaney and Muldoon, but how true to the spirit of 'Recent Irish Poetry' and its 'rupture of the lines of communication' would it be if these writers had only to name-check Beckett to prove their credentials? To honour Beckett's poetics of counter-fecundity is to submit to the miscarriage of the various assumptions of identity, language and selfhood on which so much discussion of Irish poetry still depends. As long as arguments for the poetry of Trevor Joyce or Catherine Walsh, to take only those two names, are presented under the aegis of an 'antiquarians and others' divide, we implicitly concede the stage to a hostile lyric tradition, whose dominance this terminology only serves to reinforce. Thus we might agree with

John McAuliffe that 'A couple of variant forms of Irish modernism have redawned so often now that their time seems to be always "now" and "gone"', but if we substitute 'Irish lyric tradition' for 'Irish modernism' that sentence haemorrhages meaning while making an essentially identical claim. Under this argument the lyric tradition is simply there, in place, as of right, while the modernist tradition must endlessly present and re-present its credentials in the hope of acceptance. The blame for this binary thinking may lie not just with us but the 'antiquarians and others' divide in the first place, but had the war announced in 'Recent Irish Poetry' been winnable it may have interested Beckett less. In the words of an ultra-short late poem, 'bail bail till better / founder', the bifurcative 'founder' of the last line being a moment of capsizing rather than foundation.

One small step towards a more Beckettian poetics would be the expansion, which is to say mongrelisation, of the Irish poetic genepool to include writers neither born nor based in Ireland but who nevertheless engage with the Irish condition, on whatever terms or grounds. Conspicuous among these is Susan Howe, a writer with Becket connections of her own. Howe apprenticed at the Gate Theatre in 1955, and in her 2003 collection *The Midnight* pays tribute to her mother Mary Manning Howe, who had worked at that theatre twenty years before, where she attempted to recruit Beckett to help her with the dialogue of her play *Youth's the Season.* Despite or because of this family connection, Howe has refrained from writing about Beckett in her poetry. In the final section of *The Midnight*, Howe writes:

A fugitive near the cold
coast hear what you call
'my story' such as it is
Propitious wanton snow
you and I are one Orphan
Narrow footpath for two
Pay no rent to soothe me
Spook of a field isled out
Quick live in my heart I
will trace things things

As in Beckett's *Company*, a voice comes to one in the second person, addressing us with a promise of 'my story' that may or may not be the hoped-for tale of our lives at last. The hearer is a fugitive being, in a zone of cold and snow, a fellow orphan in a constricting zone of no fixed tenancy. The landscape is reminiscent of the opening *Text for Nothing*, whose speaker lies in a mountain quag. I began with the Leibnizian monads of Hugh MacDiarmid's sperm, each alone in its own island existence or 'spook of a field isled out', but to say 'you and I are one Orphan' is also to say 'you and I are one'. In spite of the obstacles Beckett places in the way of poetic interlocutors, Howe's return to 1930s Ireland enters into a jubilant dialogue with the Beckett line – showing it can be done – furthering and expanding it, offering it a boggy shelter that will say to its fugitive ghost, 'Quick live in my heart', together to 'trace things things'.

He Alone Shall Be Called Weather

Caoilinn Hughes

I will show you fear in a handful of dust
– T.S. Eliot

The soil had been reached
down into
for its wet –
yolk beneath the flour mixture.
The ground had been worked like a beloved
bible to get through to
the deepdown democratic
scorch-douse cycle
that was unfailable as the great
White house, the great Wall
Street, Hims sung in Mississippi.
On-the-wagon-off-the-
wagon spells repeat
just like atoners wrongs're
righted (even when the offsetting
happens out of view, way up where,
way up out of the way the way Earth
has poker hot water at its core.
Don't have to see it to know it's there.)
Don't have to wonder if the ocean will tide
out again after the spring high roller.
Pray away for it
but it will come round
when it comes right.
Meantime, birdies fly south.

Still, there'd been too much wheat
in war diets, undue sun, such hope held
on skylines, givens, the determination of
                                    elbows. Then,
in the summer of thirty-one,
the rain failed.

Lakes bowed low
as if in ungainly foreign custom.
The thousand years it had taken the land
to compound an inch of topsoil, the wind
                                  whipped up
more than a mile of in less than a trice.
They recited: When rain falls.
No respite but in grits.
Flare-up letup let it be so long 's He wills it.
Pickrel ran over his own mail
box when the hundred million acre expanse
                                  of prairie
 – the Southern Plains –
came down to his hand in front of his eyes.
Automobile sandblasted to steel fundamentals,

plough and reaper. He had become immune
to the halo of its electric shock, as if to the
accumulation scumming his infant's eyes shut.
He groped through the dust drift for his doorstep.

Jensen's palms were devout:
May peace flow quickly into rivers.
He would do without the clean rises
of bread, woman's figure, hot-ironed
sheets, sacs of grain like so much
pleasure, plenty, well-oiled hair,
if it rains. His wife was lost
to the shoulder through holes cut into cloth
so that she could knead
dough in a dresser without the flour-fine silt
bleeding in bolshie red. It was enough
that the loess wore down their teeth.
They fed in a hurry and at once
before its claim was laid.
If it rains, they prayed.

They drank milk in nips from sealed Mason jars.
The cattle's udders had dried
along with their feed, their heft,
lungs weighing heavy as four stomachs.
Gauze-masked, bleak-phlegmed, the childer
drew each other's double-barreled
names on their quilts
when they wheezed themselves awake. They believed
the Great Obscure Dusk beneath their beds
would boil up and out as a black ghoul
rising thousands of feet into the sky,
transmogrifying day to night; would
suck up swoop over storm millions of tons
of dirt through their lives; brew the landscape
to tea-like murk; would swallow tractors horses trees
dream-catchers shacks net pay tackle fence-
rows retributions all hope of possessions but not
the chickens who would shuffle into coops
deeming Sky to have fallen.
Some Joe musta done mighty wrong.
Spates of jackrabbits and locusts on top it of all
were not for nothing. If it rains,
they adjured together.
He alone shall be called Weather.

Oklahoma outshone one hundred degrees
for thirty-seven slow days of thirty-four.
The wind moved snow-like alluvian, half-
engulfing houses. Grown women had to climb
out of windows with shovels and petitions.
You gave us beer. Now give us water.
They hung drenched sheets crosswise,
stuffing the frames with gummed tape
and kerchiefs. Some sealed their homes
so tight, kerosene lamps doused them –
kin, comfort, pith – odorlessly, colourless.

Wind blew for twenty-seven days and nights
in the spring of thirty-five without end. A man
by the name of Hankel saw a truck whooshed
fifty yards along the yellow sand road like tin.
Hoffman's alfalfa seeds were long blown out of
the ground and he troubled at his wife's
shallow grave. Nothing grew for a garland.
He cut silk flowers from her bridal gown;
thumbed them auburn.
Manmade petals autumn early.

April is the cruelest month.

On the second day, the cloud
set upon Boston, Buffalo, Chicago, and all along
the alphabet to Washington, D.C.
Oceanliners were coated in dust like open casket
ship models in smalltown museums.
Hugh Hammond Bennett made his plea to congress,
pointing at a muted sun through the stained glass:
This, gentlemen, is what I have been talking about.
And so, the shadow was lifted together with the doubt.
Substantiation upon Ford bonnets.
Transubstantiation upon their tongues
o'er, once the agronomy was reformed.
The tremendous national awakening transpired
within the month: a Bill passed, payed, for closure.
Human folly had been the sin, yes indeed, but it had been
in the right spirit: Work
into the direction of the Dream.
Roosevelt ordered a belt
of two-hundred million trees to be planted
from Canada to Texas to break
the wind, hold water in the soil,
keep hold of the earth –
albeit to come, not the earth that had been,
gone—to educate farmers.
Plough into the direction of the wind.

But there was no going back.
Everything those people knew
they had piled into their jalopies.
It had got so black.
Boys, girls, friends, relatives.
When it rains.

{{du|he|tao}} A sequence
Eric Langley

I.

{{ You stand in the Linshui marketplace,
among rows of shell on shell:
trying to make
a chance. }}

Tap: just when I'm all hulled up
all crabbed in confine
comes your unexpected
crick and nap and crack,
smart sound of tough love
on my round nutshell,
the flex and squeezed pop
of steely hap-crackers
snapped on infinite space.

Your husky insinuations
tend to my shelly cave;
you apply your callipers
and the heartnut aches.

You ground around it
lick soft sound
right round it
give lip up down it:
you take your breaks,
make flouts and entry-touts,
flushed over and out
quite tight to the fine fractures.

II.

{{ Fetch Felix with his nine lives!
Here come the Radical Squad:
Trojans on their
long walk. }}

Tap: you side-step
racked hair-triggers,
drip-lines, trip-
wire now silly-strung
all green-lit, defused
overlines out across
my active areas: and so
no bang, no bang.

III.

{{ He made ink from crushed walnuts,
drawing a foetus in utero,
and studies of birds:
'if there is no love,
what then?' }}

Groan us quite together
tight till pips speak;
grind to find the
white sincerity
of sliced bread-and-butter.

Sure, there is a kernel of some
mattered thing
in here and understood
if only you can eat it
and make it matter much.

Every tale, told to tend;
every seed, on-the-nail,
palpably pecked
just so
remotely touched.

Your smoothed ectoderm
moves between my hushed lips
my chapped seams;
your horn bill chirrups,
demand response,
insisting payment, up and out,
my brain-pan cleft by a brown bill.

Passerine, push your bills your rosters
clear under the door
sealed in soft keratin.

So slip your keen rostrum
through my outer wall:
tap tap, rat-a-tat.

IV.

{{ *For a man's house is his castle,*
and each man's home
his safest refuge,

Click-click come release
my high-sprung tender chords,
my tight-strung relockers;
scoping out the change
scooping up the charge
with your sure fingers
touching tumblers – T5 to T8 –
tripping notches on the sternum
so so sensitive to
sleight slops in my spun dials.

Peeling back drop-locks
– pericardium through epicardium –
stripping out clocks
– myocardium through endocardium –
unshackling each blocked valve
with one eye keyhole clamped
one tip pushing whorls
through ventricle and hardplate.

Twenty-one thousand nervous times
or seventy-two times per minute
is all in all it takes
on autodial
and I'm outstunned
hot-lanced on such hot thermals
such hot vena cava such hot chordae.

And if all else fails
take this safe
take this heart

and just
bounce it
all the way
down stairs.

That should flick the trips
turn tricks, click clicks.

V.

so particular and
so tender. }}

O, O, O, Peterman,
although I'm glad to see you
doing your job,
you beak intruder,
you superthief, you
barefoot dinnertime bandit,
don't think on a white instant
that I don't apprehend you,
loafing around, stealing about,
pilfering the shopfloor
of *Bertha's Gift & Home Furnishings*,
violin under one arm,
and *Tete de Femme*, the other.

I left the door ajar,
broken for entry,
predisposed
for your hot-prowl,
for your calling card
on my welcome-mat.

VI.

{{ -sh | -shh | -shhh
no words, no words
hush hush
-sh }}

Tap tap: as Bourne-shell shifts
on crushed Korn-shell
as softly C-shells born
again to Bash, and
as the grit gets in
clean through
clear to
the snagged heartstone,
I dare to hope you may
just see
it's me | concisely.

Shortcut to me
shortcut sent to you
in a shared moment
of sheer felicity,
spliced standard-to-offbeat,
dragged out along
my leading edges
across platforms
into new contexts
and laid out
relational.

{{ *Give me that man and I will wear him*
at heart's core, ay in my heart of heart,
as I do thee:
hush }}

Until at last, with apple pie,
with plum pudding,
and eye-spy-glass,
cased up *hús*
in their paper bag,
you came clean
to the little house
to its open door,
to tease the drawback
to cut the head
to part the charge,
 the hot cloud
 the hot cloud
 the hot crowd of
 thermal swarmed electron
 of eased atomic orbital
 in gradient still and
 radiating

Sweet remnant,
wear right through
the core-wall,
hold fast to
the heart of hearts
– *au cœur du corps* –
dismantle, drill,
go crash go dump,
and strip back insulation
to take each cord and twist
 each threaded twine
 each high-fibered hawser-line
 teased out on the heartrope
 scoped tight to find
 the red electric
 ravelling

VIII.

{{ *Lin Changzhu stands, whistling to the air,*
alone in the marketplace at Linshui,
out among the laminar ranks
of shell and shell and shell:
you pays, you takes
your choice your
chance }}

Du he tao: we're out here
just betting on skin.

Come, slice right though it –
cute through cupule –
and let's see what we've got.

I'm all out here: gambling.

An English walnut or *nux Gallica*?
mopan-mopan or mother-child?
a dud, a duff? dog-throw ratscrew
slapjack snap (tap-tap)
a right fine pair.

This one: a government official's hat,
a chicken's heart, a lantern: that.

And you're twisted in
doubled up, front-run vigorish
for the vulture or the Venus throw:
skin in the game, pounds of it.

Now on the nutshell
stick the knife-drop on
capsule's tender acupoint,
clip point to the tense yield strain
to track tip through
hawkpoint keen to kerf
and trailing
wanton slipped swarf
in surfy cream curls
and open out and out and up:
and there

it's me

sat with a crimped copy of Homer,
and a lucky cricket.

I am, it seems, rolled round
palmed around
worth the punting
gambolled smooth
all good in circulation
just hap and unconfined:
nothing to be
frayed by.

IX.

{{ *So with one finger, press-by-press,*
arm stretched out of bed,
I type out slow happen
stance on keywater
brightboarding,

while you
sleep. }}

MA in Creative Writing

An exciting new programme at Durham University

Taught by award-winning writers
Dr Paul Batchelor and Dr Vidyan Ravinthiran

Full-time and Part-time pathways
in Poetry and Prose Fiction

Academically rigorous course

One of the UK's leading English Departments:
ranked 1st in *The Times* and *Sunday Times*
Good University Guide 2016

For more information:
www.durham.ac.uk/english.studies
paul.batchelor@durham.ac.uk
0191 334 3134

Durham
University

Reviews

Prismatic Subdivisions

The New Concrete: Visual Poetry in the 21st Century
Edited by Chris McCabe & Victoria Bean
Hayward Publishing 2015

Reviewed by Oliver Dixon

Submerged within the hermetic prose of Mallarmé's 1897 preface to 'Un Coup de Des Jamais N'Abolira le Hasard' is a tentative prognostication of what might emerge in the future from his seminal typographic 'score': *almost an art-form*. The phrase acknowledges the poem's radical deployment of visual aspects of the text – spacing, letter-size, 'variable positions' of lines of different lengths up and down the page, the 'blancs' (both blanks and whitenesses) given their due importance – to initiate 'prismatic subdivisions of the Idea': meaning is suspended 'in hypothesis', linear narrative evaded and a sense of the poem's imaginative drift 'flowers and rapidly disperses according to the mobility of the writing'.

What Mallarmé could hardly have foreseen is the fecundity and diversity with which this hybrid form continues to evolve, as amply evidenced in *The New Concrete: Visual Poetry in the 21st Century*. The reason 'Un Coup de Des' – alongside that contrasting scalpel of Symbolist language-dissection, Rimbaud's 'Voyelles' – stands at the head of subsequent achievements in the field of concrete poetry, such as those found in Bean and McCabe's illuminating anthology, is Mallarmé's concept of orchestrated visual components being as integral to poetic meaning as semantic ones and his foresight into how this could redefine the act of reading.

There is a sense, of course, in which all poetry could be considered concrete, since the two chief attributes which differentiate poetic discourse from prose are firstly that it has a visual dimension in its layout on the page and secondly that through its concerted use of a range of phonetic and rhetorical devices it foregrounds the materiality of its own language, renders the words that habitually pass us by in the fugitive, unstable flow of speech and daily news more concrete; more (in Pound's phrase) 'charged with meaning'.

We live in an age where, thanks to an increasingly seamless interface between media, mass-marketing and the internet, we are surrounded by more textual information than at any other time in history, and yet this monetising saturation leaches the most part of the language around us of its human content and context. Logos, slogans and taglines grasp our attention less for what their words say than for how they look, their connotative impact in relation to other visual data. By taking advantage of the same paralinguistic elements and working from angles outside the increasingly rarefied margins print-based poetry finds itself in, the 'new concrete' is able to *detourne* the empty verbiage of consumerism back on itself, while in its incisive minimalism (as Kenneth Goldsmith suggests in his cogent introduction) 'it seems designed for short attention-spans'.

Concrete or visual poetry, however, is not a recent phenomenon: shape-poems have in fact existed as far back as the Greek Anthology and in many instances since where a poem has been inscribed on a piece of jewellery or an altar and has had to follow the restricted space of the object's design. The wing-stanzas of George Herbert, the *carmina figurata* of Renaissance poets and the 'calligrammes' of Apollinaire have at least the mimetic guiding-principle of visually rhyming with their subject-matter, unlike the more arbitrary and cutaneous visual effects of ee cummings.

In fact cummings – in attempting to lend a veneer of modernity to what were mostly hackneyed post-Romantic lyrics by de-capitalising them and playing with their punctuation and layout – was merely responding to a favourable *zeitgeist* (his first volume *Tulips and Chimneys* appeared in 1923). In the ferment of new ideas and movements whipped up by the First World War, literary and art-practice interbred and cross-pollinated with unprecedented vigour, leading to a tendency common to Cubists, Futurists and Dadaists of treating text as visual imagery to be cut up, re-aligned and defamiliarised. The typographically-rich linguistic vortex of Joyce's *Ulysses* and the ideogrammatic methodology of Pound's early *Cantos*, as well as numerous other Modernist experiments, are of a piece with this 'revolution of the word'.

It wasn't until 1956 in Sao Paolo, however, that concrete poetry as an actual movement and a theoretical approach arose, founded by the Noigandres group consisting mainly of the brothers Haroldo and Augusto de Campos (poetic cousins, perhaps, of Alvaro de Campos, Pessoa's most prolific heteronym). It was a passage in *Canto XX*, in fact, that gave rise to the group's name: in it Pound recounts how he went to visit an expert on Provencal troubadour-poetry called 'old Levi' and asks him about a word he'd been unable to translate:

'Yes, Doctor, what do they mean by *noigandres*?'
And he said: Noigandres! NOIgandres!
'You know for seex mon's of my life
'Effery night when I go to bett, I say to myself:
'Noigandres, eh, *noi*gandres,
'Now what the DEFFIL can that mean!'

A mysterious, untranslatable term from an unfamiliar language, repeated in this passage to the point where it starts breaking down into mere sound, seems an appropriate name for this movement straddling art and literature, with an agenda of creating 'a visual Esperanto that would ultimately dissolve linguistic – and thereby political – barriers between nations' (Goldsmith). By investing new revolutionary zeal into foundering late Modernism from its Developing World perspective, the Noigandres in fact instigated a thriving international scene in concrete poetry throughout the late fifties and sixties, whose incursion into the staid climate of post-war British poetry was grudgingly registered via the linguistic hinterland of Scotland: although under-appreciated in London, Edwin Morgan and Ian Hamilton Finlay (the latter included in this anthology) proved themselves concrete poets of global stature.

After a period of abeyance during the decades after this heyday, concrete poetry has enjoyed a significant resurgence in the twenty-first century, as *The New Concrete* attests. The collection's very status as a large, thick, beautifully-reproduced art-book – and huge credit must go to Hayward Publishing for the high standard and quality of this elegantly-designed volume, visually appealing before you even begin to examine the poems – speaks of its scope and range beyond the print-bound limitations of most poetry books. It's the variety and multi-faceted nature of what one discovers inside, furthermore, which is so intriguing, from the ultra-minimalism of Thomas A Clark and Julie Johnstone (recalling Mallarmé's incorporation of whitenesses) to the denser word-swarms of Donato Mancini, Jordan Abel and Natalie Czech. In each case, the poet/artist has contributed a brief explicatory comment on their piece, invariably guiding the reader without imposing a unitary meaning on these highly open-ended texts.

It's also fascinating to note the convergence here between poets whose work has appeared in more conventional formats, such as Susan Howe, John Kinsella, Sean Bonney and Chris McCabe himself, and visual artists such as Tom Phillips, Sue Tompkins and Vito Acconci, whose work might more often be encountered in a gallery. Traditional antinomies between writers and artists are breaking down in the field of visual poetry, in other words, and an energising traffic of ideas and inspirations is moving between them. *The New Concrete* provides excellent contextual materials for further explorations: not only Goldsmith's introduction but interesting essays by Bean and McCabe on how they compiled the collection, as well as notes on contributors and an invaluable set of pertinent quotations on concrete poetry at the front and back of the book.

'I would give you Leaves of Grass...'

Stevie Smith
Collected Poems and Drawings of Stevie Smith
ed. & introduced by Will May
Faber and Faber
£35 (hb)

Reviewed by Rebecca Watts

There can't be many poets whose collected works, issued in an academically rigorous and handsomely produced hardback volume, have the potential to give a reviewer bad dreams; perhaps Stevie Smith is the only one. Certainly, Will May's fresh survey of the eight poetry collections Smith prepared for publication (along with a substantial batch of hitherto uncollected poems and thirty pages of previously unpublished poems) is a testament to the uniqueness of her art.

Faithful to the presentation of the individual collections, the book allows plenty of space for Smith's unobstructive language and striking line drawings to work their strange magic. As May notes, the illustrations 'are as likely to put us on our guard as provide relief'; they rarely display any clear relationship to the poems' content, and the majority despite their apparent playfulness exude a sinister quality. The thin paper characteristic of Faber's newer collected editions has here the bonus effect of creating ghost illustrations, as figures belonging to other poems can be seen sneaking about through the pages, intensifying the already unsettling atmosphere of the poems.

In his brief, engaging introduction, May describes Smith's inconsistent approach to publication – how she 'agonised over which poems and drawings to include in individual books', yet happily 'changed words, titles or illustrations to dodge copyright issues' and would decide which version of a published poem to reprint in a collection based on which newspaper could supply the copy first. She also habitually amended poems in her reading and performance copies but hardly ever passed the revisions on to her editors. May uses Smith's 'amended final versions' as his source texts, documenting their differences from the original published versions in his notes at the back of the volume. While these primarily serve an academic purpose, they shed light on a poetic personality who cared greatly how her work would go over in performance and increasingly worried about being misinterpreted (hence her tendency to add punctuation later). Occasional references to Smith's letters, manuscripts and annotated drafts from the archives at the Universities of Tulsa and Hull provide additional sustenance for the interested reader.

Collectively the poems construct an enigmatic picture of a writer who, as May puts it, 'takes poetry seriously enough to risk not being taken seriously', who vacillates wildly between sardonic commentary and humane philosophy, witty realism and girlish abstraction. The work's defining feature is its boisterous energy, always pushing against a near-relentless morbidity. Some of this energy is the product of Smith shaking up her numerous and varied literary influences: May specifically notes Blake, Dickinson, Dorothy

Parker, Ogden Nash, Keats, Wallace Stevens and the *Golden Treasury* crew; Joyce, Eliot and the Metaphysicals are also overtly present.

Smith's formal flair shines through. She deploys the short line brilliantly to execute social satire ('Major Hawkaby Cole Macroo / Chose / Very wisely / A patient Griselda of a wife with a heart of gold [...]') and can drive a long line as surely as Whitman, whether traversing abstract ground (as in 'The Abominable Lake') or denouncing inhumane physical practices (as in 'This is Disgraceful and Abominable'). The glorious 'Dear Karl' is an overt homage to Whitman, infused with Smith's trademark mischief and bathos:

[...] If I had what hypocritical poetasters crocodilely
whining call lucre and filthy,
But man, and it takes a man to articulate the unpalatable
truth,
Means of support, if I had this and a little more,
I would give you Leaves of Grass, I would send
All of Walt Whitman to you with a smile that guesses it is
More blest to give than receive.
For I, I myself, I have no Leaves of Grass
But only Walt Whitman in a sixpenny book,
Taste's, blend's, essence's, multum-in-parvo's Walt
Whitman.
And now sending it to you I say:
Fare out, Karl, on an afternoon's excursion, on a sixpenny
unexplored uncharted road,
Over sixpennyworth of tarmac, blistered by an American
sun, over irrupted boulders,
And a hundred freakish geology's superimpositions. Fare
out on a strange road
Between lunchtime and dinner. Bon voyage, Karl, bon
voyage.

The nine-line lyric 'The Doctor' is a good example of how far Smith's poems can travel despite being rooted in a very narrow context. The opening stanza and illustration work together to construct a neat cliché of the overbearing clinician, only for the patient's response to spill out, saturated with pain but determined to transform it (via some unnerving rhyme-control) into tidy oblivion:

Yes, I find that it is more than I can bear, so give me some
bromide
And then I will go away for a long time and hide
Somewhere on the seashore where the tide

Coming upon me when I am asleep shall cover

Me, go over entirely,
Carry beyond recovery.

What starts as parody ends with the erasure of the subject – a solemn, deeply individual experience that shuts out the reader along with the world. Desire for oblivion pervades the volume; about eighty percent of the poems refer to or directly address d/Death. This grows tiresome, and when the writing does (occasionally) admit beauty it's as refreshing as a cold shower on a stifling day. A few nature-themed poems yield this effect, not least 'Pretty', where the apparent sarcasm of the refrain is undermined by the speaker's plain acceptance of nature's ways:

And it is careless, and that is always pretty
This field, this owl, this pike, this pool are careless,
As Nature is always careless and indifferent
Who sees, who steps, means nothing, and this is pretty.

In the earlier poem 'Now, Pine-Needles', a similar matter-of-factness is combined with an unmasked tenderness for its unusual object:

Well, you do not know
That you were so and so
And are now so and so.
So why should I say
You were alive and are now dead
That your parent tree sighs in the wind?

In sentiment and tone this poem borrows from the Zen Buddhists, stating and restating the facts to get to a metaphysical truth and, in the process, achieving acceptance: 'I will sleep on you pine-needles, / Then I shall be / No more than the pine-tree / No more than the pine-tree's needles.' Though its gentle serenity is unusual for Smith, the poem's thesis, that all things tend towards decay, is an obsession and a driving force across her work.

As her most-anthologised poems ('Not Waving but Drowning', 'Pad, pad', 'Bog-Face') demonstrate, Smith has an acute talent for compressing biographies, psychologies and philosophies into neat lyrics. As a style which hides its artistry this can come across as cold and glib. Over time, though, the poems' implicit meanings and eerie atmospheres have a tendency to expand. Like the 'savage' tiger skin's effect on the defenceless infant in 'The Photograph', exposure to Smith's *Collected Poems and Drawings* is likely to leave a deep, discomforting impression.

Reading English

Andrew Crozier, *'Free Verse' as Formal Restraint: An Alternative to Metrical Conventions in Twentieth Century Poetic Structure* (Shearsman) £14.95

Harriet Tarlo, *Poems 2004-2014* (Shearsman) £9.95

Reviewed by Ian Seed

Peter Riley wrote that 'there have been few writers whose radicalism went to the roots of language's relationship to experience as that of Andrew Crozier' (www.theguardian.com/books/2008/jul/21/culture.obituaries). Yet until recently much of his work was out of print or scattered in small press publications. In 2012, Ian Brinton edited *A Crozier Reader* (Carcanet), a selection of Crozier's poetry and prose, and in 2013 *Thrills and Frills: Selected*

Prose (Shearsman). Brinton has now edited an unpublished early critical work for Shearsman. It makes for a fascinating complementary volume. From Brinton's Introduction, we learn that this work was Crozier's PhD thesis, presented to the University of Essex in 1973. His examiner was J.H. Prynne.

Crozier begins thus:

My intention in writing this thesis has been to cast some light on the *prima facie* case that free verse, in abandoning the exercise of metre, has abandoned that principle of restraint upon which the creation of artistic form depends. This point of view contrasts with a general contention on the part of the exponents of free verse that their works possess form which is not only unique but which also bears an immediate relation to the significance of the work, a relationship felt to be 'musical', although not in any directly analogical sense. (p. 13)

He makes his case through an examination of discussions of poetic theory and notions of rhythm and metre that have taken place in English poetry since the sixteenth century. It is not enough, Crozier points out, to look only at the radical changes that took place in 1908. Rather, we need to see these in the context of the 'steady, evolutionary march of English poetry' (p. 16). Throughout this examination, Crozier divides poetic theories into two kinds: on the one hand those that take a more superficial approach, which, however useful at a technical level, do not get down to the real business of poetry; and on the other hand, those which conduct a proper enquiry into the authentic purpose and work of poetry, which is to establish the place of humankind in relation to the universe, and ultimately, in theological terms, to God. A superficial account would posit

an ideal sonnet-form, say, which is a fiction designed to enable us to recognise whether a certain poem is or is not a member of the class 'sonnet' and, if it is found to be a member of this class, to say how well it observes the rules for that class of object [...]. It relegates formal considerations to a level at which they can be merely assumed [...] or transformed into the idea of genre, thus releasing the critic to attend to his 'real' business of discussing 'meaning' and making him the artist's peer. (p. 35)

A detailed example given of this kind of criticism is that of Yvor Winters, for whom 'structure, form and detail all depend on the existence and observation of convention [...] the poetic line is neither a semantic nor a syntactic unit, but a unit of measurement' (p. 37). Against this, Crozier wishes to 'see if it is possible to envisage alternative modes of poetic organisation on the basis of attention to the full range of phonetic items in language without reducing them to selective metrical sets (pp. 41–2). After investigating Pound's notion of 'absolute rhythm' (to which he returns in the final pages of this book) and after distinguishing this notion from the poetics of Pound's contemporaries, such as Hulme, Flint and Eliot, Crozier creates a genealogy stretching back to the sixteenth-century Humanists (not to be confused with current-day

atheists), who sought to 'appeal to a musical concordance between man, poetry, the structure of the cosmos, and the Divine Will' (p. 97). People such as Campion, Ascham, and of course Milton, expressed a contempt for rhyme, which was perceived as 'barbarous and rude'. The rhythms of poetry should return humankind to its true nature, whether understood in a theological framework or in a more secular sense in the age of the Enlightenment.

The final chapter of *Free Verse* brings us to Crozier's conclusion that 'although it is a circumstance of regret to many people, language is not a pure symbolic system, not a system of fixed and fiduciary symbols, not defined by the relation of signifier to signified' (p. 193). Not an unusual claim perhaps. However, he goes on to say that if we see language in this limited way, it will be 'effectively deprived' of its 'authentically sensory character' (p. 201). Poetry, through its exercise of language, 'offers the fullest account possible of what we experience' (p. 205). The techniques and rhythms of 'free verse' allow the skilled poet to 'objectively' reflect the complexities of humankind's experience. In this way, the use of technique becomes a 'proof' of the poet's sincerity.

Crozier's arguments are complex, and as Prynne noted in his report, there is at times 'a lack of clarity'. This brief review cannot do justice to these complexities, or convey the pleasure to be taken in reading Crozier's survey and examination of poetic theory over the last five centuries, whether or not one agrees with everything he says. *'Free Verse' as Formal Restraint* is a book which has to be read.

⁓

Harriet Tarlo's poems could be regarded as a kind of enactment of Pound's 'absolute rhythm'. In Tarlo's use of spaces and sounds, language becomes a sensory experience along with the landscapes she explores. Her work can be seen as part of a new wave of 'radical landscape' poetry which has emerged over the last decade or so, remaking the pastoral and working out of a modernist tradition which includes poets such as Basil Bunting, Charles Olson, Ian Hamilton Finlay and Lorinne Niedecker. It represents a bold attempt to break down the barriers between words and things, human beings and nature, subject and object.

Tarlo invites the reader to live through experience with her, but at no point is there an obvious attempt to seduce the reader. The title of her book, *Poems 2004–2014* (following on from her *Poems 1990–2003*), is itself perhaps a refusal to deliberately catch the eye of anyone who is potentially interested. Her poetry takes on a highly ethical, and dare I say it, almost puritanical stance in its uncompromising aesthetic. The lyrical 'I' almost (but not quite) disappears. The concentration is all on the object, person, situation or landscape being observed. However, none of this makes her work any less delightful to read.

'Relations', the first section of the book, is where the 'I' is most present, but always secondary to the sounds of words and their associations, and to the spaces created around her use of imagery, with an emphasis on the senses. The tone is generally tender, but avoids sentimentality:

child sleeping   sweating into
her skin   full length   face down
on her torso   not a baby, a boy
coiling curls salty   spring   his
pores open   voices outside are
nothing   pushing up   his eyes
flick a second

                    ('flush')

In a manner reminiscent of the early William
Carlos Williams, there is a delight in small things
that we would normally pay little attention to, for
example 'pencil shavings'

falling   each
            here
            still

                ('graphite')

However, in the case of Tarlo, these things are
usually seen in the context of a much wider
landscape, so that in the poem just quoted from,
we begin with:

sea-layers   sky
                seeing sky   as sea
                        stretched over
        wide sweep   pale   skin   cliff

The effect is that of looking at a landscape picture,
and then stepping much closer, or rather inside,
to observe, and live with, the pleasure of a tiny
detail. To borrow from Heidegger's terminology,
we are awakened to the beingness of being.

'Place-time', the second section of *Poems*,
consists mainly of a series of observations, which
can be coolly scientific at times, or subjectively
impressionistic at others (though, as mentioned

above, the 'I' for the most part remains excluded
– the poet is not concerned here with expressing
her feelings). They work like a series of exquisite
photos, permeated with a quiet beauty:

        tall nettle tops   tremble-out

up Trow Gill closing in under single
limestone drips   full dawn comes
in the face of the hill, the lee of morning
shaded down   distant grass holds
day's sunlight

                ('6.30am, 15 Oct 2011')

Tarlo also makes use of found text for her poems.
For example, the first section of her poem 'An
English House' consists entirely of what seem to
be notices associated with Bretton Hall in West
Yorkshire. Here we are made acutely yet subtly
aware of the centuries-old wealth and power
which lie behind any country estate that we enjoy
visiting. The last section of her book, 'enviro', is
more overtly political in the way it raises issues
connected to the ecology of our planet and the
disparities of wealth and living standards in the
world. For example, an 84-year old Malawi villag-
er's experience of flooding is in stark contrast to
those of us who are

so glad we went to Spain this year
to see the sun shining in its morning
glory through the bougainvillea
get away from all this rain

                ('Friday Piece')

The poetry of Harriet Tarlo does not offer
any easy solutions, but rather challenges
us to think for ourselves about the kinds of
choices and commitments we must make.

Elysium on Earth

Yevgeny Baratynsky
Half-light & Other Poems
bilingual edition, translated
and with an introduction by
Peter France
Arc Publications, 2015
£9.99

Reviewed by Boris Dralyuk

For decades, in the absence of inspired trans-
lations, it was nearly impossible to convince
Anglophone readers of Alexander Pushkin's genius.
One could make all the claims one wanted, but
there was simply no way to prove them. Slowly
but surely, the case for Pushkin improved. The
poet's defenders can now muster hard evidence,
including Stanley Mitchell's sparkling recreation
of *Eugene Onegin* (2008). But how much worse the
situation has been for Pushkin's brilliant contem-
poraries. Konstantin Batyushkov (1787–1855),

Pyotr Vyazemsky (1792–1878), and Yevgeny Bara-
tynsky (1800–1844) remain virtually unknown
outside Russia. One hopes that Peter France's
sensitive and graceful translations of Baratynsky,
whom he compares to Giacomo Leopardi in both
spirit and stature, will finally win Pushkin's most
original and accomplished peer an appreciative
readership in the Anglophone world.

Baratynsky, for his part, was prepared to wait. A
brief lyric of 1828 expresses – and demonstrates
– the modesty of his aspirations and the austerity
of his vision:

My talent is pitiful, my voice not loud,
but I am living; somewhere in the world
someone looks kindly on my life; far off
a distant fellow-man will read my words
and find my being; and, who knows, my soul
will raise an echo in his soul, and I
who found a friend in my own time,
will find a reader in posterity.

Born into a noble family, Baratynsky seemed dest-
ined for a career as an officer, but he was expelled

from the Page Corps for an act of theft – likely a schoolboy prank. He spent a couple years in the countryside, steeped in the melancholy that would haunt him throughout his life, and there began to write. At nineteen he decided to redeem himself the hard way, entering the army as a private, and a few years later established a literary reputation with a long Romantic poem, *Eda* (1824), and his elegiac, ruminative lyrics.

Pushkin famously praised Baratynsky as the only poet in his circle who 'thinks', and Baratynsky's work is often described as 'philosophical'. As France suggests in his eloquent introduction, however, 'philosophical' should not be taken to mean coldly rational, abounding in profound, fixed ideas. What strikes one most about Baratynsky is the immediacy of his thought.

In the poet's greatest collection, *Half-light*, the reader sees and feels Baratynsky thinking, often painfully and reluctantly ('Thought, yet more thought!'). By the time of its release in 1842, this kind of meditative poetry was out of fashion; though happily married, he had lived an intellectually isolated life for a number of years, finding solace in his craft:

In the dark sleep of lifelessness,
amid the world's sepulchral cold,
the poet finds some joy, sweet rhyme,
in your caress, in you alone!
You, like the faithful dove, bring back
a green branch to the waiting ark
and place it in his eager hand;
you only with your echoing voice

give inspiration a human face
and bring his dream to land.

('Rhyme')

Baratynsky died in 1844 in Naples, and France's selection ends with an ecstatic ode to the 'Steamship' (1844), written at sea, in which the poet proclaims: 'Tomorrow I see Elysium on earth!' This Whitmanesque celebration of modern existence is tragic; it comes at the very close of Baratynsky's life, a glimmer of optimism that contrasts sharply with the bleak perspective of his earlier years. 'Ultimate Death' (1828), for instance, is a harrowing prophecy of man's fatal withdrawal from nature into 'the hands of fantasy', and of nature's subsequent reclamation of the world – a vision closer to that of Robinson Jeffers than of Whitman.

Neglected for decades, Baratynsky was important to both Akhmatova and Brodsky. Perhaps a less likely advocate was Varlam Shalamov (1907–1982), whose *Kolyma Tales* chronicle his experiences in the Gulag. In a lyric poem from 1949, Shalamov wrote of discovering a volume of Baratynsky in an abandoned hut. The foreword went to a fellow convict, to be used 'for cigarette paper', the notes at the back went to another, 'for playing cards'. Shalamov, meanwhile, kept 'those precious jottings, / the dreams of a poet / now long forgotten'.[1] This was the prize, the living thoughts of an uncommon mind. Peter France's masterful translations now allow Anglophone readers to encounter that mind for themselves.

1 Varlam Shalamov, 'Baratynsky', trans. Robert Chandler, *The Penguin Book of Russian Poetry*, ed. Chandler, Boris Dralyuk, and Irina Mashinski (London: Penguin Classics, 2015), pp. 387–88.

Old Wives' Tales

Marina Tsvetaeva *Milestones*, translated by Christopher Whyte (Shearsman Books 2015) £9.95

Emilia Ivancu *Washing My Hair With Nettles,* translated by Diarmuid Johnson (Parthian 2015) £8.99

Reviewed by Ross Cogan

'What is writing poetry but translating?' Marina Tsvetaeva wrote to Rilke in 1926 – a translation in which something inevitably goes missing. Fittingly, then, Tsvetaeva herself is famously difficult to translate. Her syntax is elliptical, often twisted or compressed; her metaphors dense. Poems suddenly pause and change tempo; word order is dramatically distorted.

To make matters even harder, rhyme and metre are crucial to her work (as they still are in most Russian poetry). Omit them and you lose something vital; bungle it and – especially given her extensive use of dashes – one of Russia's greatest

poets could end up sounding like a third-rate Emily Dickinson.

So Christopher Whyte is to be applauded for taking on a thankless and near-impossible task. *Milestones* (as he follows Robin Kemball in translating *Versty*) was written in 1916, when Tsvetaeva was twenty-three, and takes the form almost of a verse journal, with entries carefully dated. And his versions certainly contain some gems, for example:

Dark as a pupil, and absorbing light
as pupils do – I love you, sharp-eyed Night.

Singing's ancient mother, in your hands
the reigns of the four winds, give me a voice

to summon you, one that can sing your praise –
me, shell in which the ocean murmurs on.

This has some of her oddness, some of her passion, but also fulfils Whyte's aim of devising 'formal constraints for each translation which, while not identical with those to be found in the original, had an analogous function.'

Sadly, such gems are rare. 'Women poets in particular have been moved by the violence of her emotions and the ferocity of her expression', says Elaine Feinstein in the 1993 edition of her *Selected Poems.* Yet the Tsvetaeva who emerges from these translations can sound more like a middle-aged Victorian clergyman. Would the young woman in the high-necked Edwardian silk gown who gazes from the cover really have written 'Just when you take your constitutional / beside the Neva' or 'my ears hearken to you' (*Poems to Blok: 5*) or 'fine featured, righteous in the eyes of God, / you, silent luminary of my soul' (*Poems to Blok: 3*)?

In Feinstein's sharper translation this last becomes 'Saint of God, beautiful, you / are the quiet light of my soul'. But perhaps Feinstein has taken liberties? The flatness of Whyte's versions might be justified if they're more literal. Yet, ironically, the opposite seems more often the case. Consider this: 'garlanded with tenderness / enfolded in the singer's arms' (p. 33). In Feinstein's version, however, the speaker is 'here, on the ribs of the singer'. In fact, the key word is груди and it means 'chest'. Neither, then, renders the meaning exactly, but Feinstein is closer. And what would possess you to reach for the cliché of enfolding arms, when you could have the hard precision of Feinstein's rib?

I can quote other, similar infelicities. Of course,

Feinstein's versions aren't without their faults. For now, though, they remain my first choice.

Emilia Ivancu is a Romanian poet, translator and critic. In *Washing My Hair With Nettles,* which is translated by Diarmuid Johnson (and presumably accurate, since the pair have cooperated for some years) we are promised a side of the region's culture 'largely unknown to readers of Western literature'. While the resulting versions occasionally veer off into a dangerously new-agey-sounding spirituality ('man is a boat / Rocking gently between past errors and others soon to be committed') on balance this is an enjoyable, interesting collection, which creates haunting effects by employing folk motifs that seem at once familiar and unfamiliar:

The horse and ox unchained,
Began to dance in circles
Telling old wives' tales to the wise,
Flowers turned to buds
And green branches sprouted on the roofs.

If your view of Romanian poetry is framed by the jovial ironies of Marin Sorescu, you may be surprised by these lush landscapes, alive with myth.

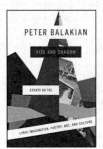

'Dangerous times / see clearly'

Peter Balakian *Ozone Journal*
(University of Chicago Press)

Peter Balakian *Vise and Shadow: Essays on the lyric imagination, poetry, art, and culture* (UCP)

Reviewed by Jamie Osborn

Peter Balakian's new collection of poems, *Ozone Journal*, revisits concerns that have occupied his work in the past. The legacy and memory of the Armenian Genocide, coming of age in well-off New England in the sixties and seventies, the nature of the past itself, are framed within such events as the Vietnam War or Prince Charles's visit to the 'slum drummers' of Nairobi. Like the flexible prosody, the style is elliptical and can at turns be tough, disorienting, or flash into moments of beauty, and Balakian deploys a characteristic historical sensitivity and well-moderated irony in splicing his materials together. The long title poem is plural, multi-layered, the past entering the present only as much as the present illuminates the past. If there is a single central impulse to 'Ozone Journal', it might lie in the quotation from Walter Benjamin, which occurs in the poem half as remembered words, half as sudden new thought: *'To articulate the past historically does not to mean to recognize it the way it really was. It means to seize hold of a memory as it flashes up at a moment of danger.'*
Balakian interweaves Benjamin's words with

flickers of Boston after midnight, song lyrics, and a voice and body 'crammed between two kids'. The result is a mix of intense sensory, even sensual, experience and cerebral force, the verse both meditative and urgent. Balakian's long lines pick up and draw out thoughts, clauses, notes, in the rhythms of exploratory prose, then snap back at unexpected line-breaks, maintaining a gut-level as well as an intellectual tension. If some passages have the feel of notes towards a theory of the past, Balakian electrifies the theory: 'history is, as Defoe put it, "the fate of / things gives a new face to things." // I plugged that into the '80s'.

The edge of irony running through the poems – not only the title poem, but also the shorter lyrics included in the collection – is perhaps a response to an encounter with dangers or atrocities about which it seems little can be done. The title poem's various strands are infused with a sense of threat and understated futility. An elegy for a friend who died in the AIDS epidemic of the electrified eighties is also a confession of paranoia: 'I walked around between classes imagining T-4 counts'. Behind the excavation of the remains of Armenian Genocide victims in the Syrian desert, which forms the narrative point of departure for 'Ozone Journal', is the knowledge that the Genocide is still not acknowledged by Turkey and many other countries. As the book's title suggests, it is also a record of the ozone hole crisis, a journal of urgent, if never quite allocable, menace and potential displacement:

aerosols, river haze, CS gas, we moved
with whatever floats – dispersions of self and industrial
                                                    manna
the shirtless exiles walking up 158th

But if pervasive threat leads to exile, it also encourages a heightened response. In an edition of Defoe's *Journal of the Plague Year*, the poet scribbles, or finds scribbled, the words 'dangerous times / see clearly'. It is not that the subject matter of Balakian's poems is clear. The dangerous times recorded by the poems are disjointed, or compressed, or appear in flashes, and are always unsettling, 'Assad- / faced façades looking back at us'. But the poems themselves seem driven by the need to fulfil that statement-and-command: 'dangerous times / see clearly'.

The essays of *Vise and Shadow*, offer a powerful defence of the same mantra. Balakian is rightly known and admired for the ethical force of his work, and his memoir, *Black Dog of Fate*, earned him praise as 'the American conscience of the Armenian Genocide'. Some of the most sensitive and enlightening essays in this book are readings of the Armenian poets Siamanto (who was killed in the Genocide) and Yeghishe Charents (who survived, but witnessed horrific events that, Balakian shows, left a deep impression on his life and work). As well as offering audiences unfamiliar with the circumstances in which they were writing a way in to these poets, Balakian makes a powerful and important case that any reading of the poems must fully take account of the impact and nature of those circumstances. Balakian sets out definitive, sometimes provocative views – on the task of poetry to remember atrocity, for example – but his arguments, and scholarship, are borne lightly and allow the poems themselves to stand out as blazingly clear. He moves beyond simplistic divides of 'personal' versus 'political' poetry to develop notions of poetry as 'ingesting violence', an idea outlined in another essay, on 'The Poetry of Witness Problem'. The essays draw on thinking about the nature of trauma, of memory and of 'formal impersonality' in poetry written in times of extreme suffering, such as the poems included in Carolyn Forché's anthology *Against Forgetting: 20th Century Poetry of Witness* (in which Balakian's translations of Siamanto appeared).

Balakian is an advocate of the belief that he finds in Siamanto, that 'If torture unmakes human consciousness, breaks down the connection between self and other, self and world, and severs the voice, then the poem [...] can offer some ethical counterforce in the aftermath.' If readers of poetry do not all already hold this belief, deep down, then Balakian's essays – which take in Adrienne Rich, Theodore Roethke and Hart Crane as well as those classed as 'witness' poets – make an eloquent and passionate case that they ought to do so. In the process he offers new ways of thinking about 'voice' or 'self' in poetry, again going beyond simple divisions of 'personal' and 'impersonal' to explore the ways in which poetry allows 'perspectives to collide and make their own music out of a cultural and historical context, one that still resonates to the psychology of violence'.

The range of the essays extends also to re-evaluations of the Armenian-American painter Arshile Gorky, to Elia Kazan's film *America, America*, and to the writings of Primo Levi. *Vise and Shadow* is a compelling mix of literary and cultural criticism and memoir, At times acknowledged obsessions – the 'vice' of the book's title – can, from being encouragingly passionate, turn to repetitiveness, and, despite its emphasis on the political and social transformations of the era, an essay on 'Bob Dylan in Suburbia' is little more than a fan's indulgent reminiscence. But at their best – which is most of the time – Balakian's essays, like the poems, in dangerous times see clearly.

Turned to Tongue

Rod Mengham,
Chance of a Storm
Carcanet, 2015
£9.99

Reviewed by Peter Hughes

'As the wind moves over to the hop-field
I would not be seen dead in that.'

I first read Rod Mengham's work in a pamphlet in the early 1980s. Over thirty years later I admired a more substantial volume combining film stills by Marc Atkins and texts by Mengham. The impressive STILL*moving* came out from Veer in 2014 and, along with its visual impact, kept offering irresistible phrases:

'All the empty sleeves that do not salute.'
'This is the kind of accident that wins awards.'
'You are very faint. You are getting fainter. I can't hear you.'

'There are traces of heat in the air through which the memories pass.'

Now we have Mengham's *Chance of a Storm,* poems and prose poems, no pictures this time, except for the one by Marc Atkins which graces the cover. It's a photograph of storm clouds above Grimspound, the atmospheric site of a Bronze Age settlement on Dartmoor. The site was abandoned, perhaps as a consequence of climate change. The storm clouds are coming this way. Landscape is always more than landscape, just as in Mengham's work lyric is always more than lyric.

In spite of the memorable lines quoted above, Mengham's poems are not the kind which leave you with just one notable image or phrase. Individual lines and phrases often have a moving lyricism, and may seem straighforward. But they tend to be followed by new thoughts arriving at a tangent, referencing apparently unrelated matter. Tones shift suddenly, from a resonant classicism to banal contemporary cliché. So one proceeds as reader by savouring the qualities of the line to hand whilst casting around for significant connections to what comes before and after. Mengham is continually weaving a web of correspondences between the historical, the political and the mundane in order to foreground global interconnectedness generally. This writing, very much in the Modernist tradition, does not make us feel as though we are eavesdropping on an author's sensitive thoughts. It connects us to the changing world and its ambiguous, contested histories. We hear the voices of those who would pillage and those who would resist. And the orchestration is achieved with wit and beauty.

The range of reference is startling. Over a few pages we encounter Archilocus, *boustrophedon*, the Shield of Achilles, Dorothy Hewett, Grianan Ailigh, Seurat, Peter Lorre, Paolo Uccello, the streets of Cracow, and Neruda (the latter in the wonderfully titled poem '9/11 is the date when the CIA-funded coup removed the Allende government from power in Chile').

There are passages of quiet power, as if from a memorable film:

The deep, muffled explosions became clearer, the dogs are raging. Beneath the strains of an unaccompanied lament, the distant voice now seems to be that of a commentator at a school sports day.

This is from a piece called 'Five Year Plan in Four Years'. The storm is coming this way. Footage from abroad we'd noticed on the news has left the TV screens and is being enacted in the next street. The distress is that of a neighbour and the distant warlord's rant now has local representation. Here is the war.

Towards the end of this book is an eight-page poem called 'A Turn around Agnès Thurnauer', the French feminist artist. One of her best known projects was a series of large badges on which the names of male artists were changed to female versions such as Nicole Poussain, Paula Picasso and Annie Warhol. Mengham's poem begins:

One day the artist released a bird in her studio. It was never seen again but the idea of a bird settled in every painting before taking flight to the next.

[...]

We can paint an idea of invisible worlds; or leave a single planet in the lurch.

The image of the bird is partly a nod to Thurnauer's series 'Prédelle', each of which featured the image of a wing. But it is also to do with imaginative transformation, the spirit taking wing, becoming manifest. Artistic gestures which change the way we think and feel. Mengham is not interested in art which is happy to 'leave a single planet in the lurch'. His work, like that of Thurnauer, is very much engaged with transformation. Just this year he curated an exhibition at Jesus College, Cambridge in which Agnès Thurnauer made three portraits of women and hung them in the college dining room to replace three pictures of men. Mengham said in an interview, 'It's time our representations of ourselves and what we do were put in perspective'. The representations of ourselves in *Chance of a Storm* are open-ended, challenging and complex. As he says in the last line of the Thurnauer poem, 'Once you begin a text, it is never finished.'

Feminine Scripture

David Kinloch, *Some Women*
Happen*Stance*
£4.00

Reviewed by James Sutherland-Smith

Reading David Kinloch is akin to enjoying a Roman bathhouse; first the frigidarium of formidable erudition, then the delight of the tepidarium, his mastery of line and sentence, followed by the caldarium, the hot room of imagery, pun and feeling. We can return to the tepidarium for a massage with fragrant oils of form and language and perhaps there is also a pretty girl or handsome boy to provide further delights. In *Some Women* he continues to write groups of poems closely related in subject matter, following his sumptuously ekphrastic *Finger of a Frenchman* (Carcanet, 2011).

In this Happen*Stance* pamphlet he has written a group of poems in the voices of women from the Bible divided into two sections corresponding to the Old Testament and the New Testament. He

must have been extremely tempted to venture into the Apocrypha and write a poem in the voice of the Susannah harassed by those two dirty old elders. The poems are risky. Firstly, female personae created by a gay male poet might be regarded with extreme suspicion by those feminist poets who have ring-fenced feminine identity against male intrusion. Secondly, the immense popularity of Carol Ann Duffy's *The World's Wife* might cast shadow on poems which adopt a similar strategy in giving a voice to the silent women in canonical male literature and the Bible, that exemplary product of patriarchal culture.

However, Kinloch has the verbal gifts, the range of register and devices and sheer cheek to write poems which are original, moving and sexy. Kinloch begins with Lilith as Adam's first wife although she only makes a solitary appearance in the actual Bible as a demon avoided by the prophet Isaiah. However, his women are more than dutiful bearers of the sons of biblical patriarchs and have their own identities and desires. Lilith was the first female rebel, one Jewish tale claiming she wanted more variation than the missionary position. The second poem is in the voice of Cain's wife, never named nor mentioned in the Bible. Whereas Lilith speaks with a cynical, individual voice, Cain's wife is generic for the uses and abuses that men put women to; in the first verse 'I was a tiller, a sower, a hoer, a sewer', and in the second: 'Then he killed Abel and I was / a drifter, a tramper, a marcher, a prowler.'

Kinloch alternates humour with seriousness. Sarah makes fun of the biblical Abraham and Sarah, aged ninety-nine and ninety respectively when Sarah conceived a child and Rebekah makes Isaac's wife an irresistible cook. 'The poetry is in the pita', is one of several excellent jokes in this chapbook. 'Deborah' celebrates the only women judge in the Bible, before we move on to the harrowing tale of the Levite's concubine, who in the Bible story was gang-raped by men from the tribe of Benjamin in place of the Levite. The concubine was then cut into twelve pieces which were dispatched to the tribes of Israel with a demand for vengeance. Humour returns with Job's celebrity-chef daughters whom God punishes at Satan's instigation, 'set Job a test. Blow his daughters away – / they've eaten the alphabet and they never pray'. There are two virtuoso poems on

King David, the first, 'B & D', on his high jinks with Bathsheba, alliterates on the phonemes 'b' and 'd': 'David was a dirty King whose dong danced / like a weathervane, a dick like a didgeridoo. It nosed Bathsheba's bouquet, top note first / heart note next, though liked the base // note best.'

From the five poems in the second part, four feature women in the New Testament and the last poem takes for its central image the whole of the Bible. Mary Magdalene is particularly powerful and like many of Kinloch's poems is enhanced by allusion: 'and I turned to the gardener (who looked like / my husband) and I screamed "The body has gone!" / He told me to look inside. "Look within."' 'Virgin' manages to blend the Virgin Mary's account of the loss of her son with that of a woman with a gay son. Kinloch's jokiness extends to 'First Letter of the Hebrew Women to St Paul', as the Epistle to the Hebrews was almost certainly not written by the apostle.

Some Women is a collection written at the highest pitch of erudition, passion and humour. At £4.00 it's an absolute bargain.

'This love that quietly lifts'

Maitreyabandhu, *Yarn*
(Bloodaxe) £9.95

Reviewed by Chris Beckett & Isao Miura

In an article entitled 'The Value Archetype', Maitreyabandhu argues that poetry and Buddhism are part of the same spiritual discipline, a means to help us discover the 'jewel of human value'. His acclaimed first collection, *The Crumb Road*, pursued this discipline with what Sean O'Brien in the Guardian called 'a rich, melancholy modesty', in which the imperfectly remembered stories of his youth and family were told with quiet but telling detail, allowing the joys and sorrows to speak for themselves. In particular, the story of a short but intense love affair with another boy, told in a series of poems called 'Stephen', has a seering, unforgettable quality that I can only ascribe to its jewel-like honesty.

Yarn purports to be a rather different sort of book. The cover blurb quotes the OED definition of yarn as 'a long or rambling story, especially one that is implausible'. But the book is again full of affectionate, wry portraits of his siblings ('my sister was very small, her face a lantern / all her own...' – Lanterns), his mother ('my sister on my father's lap. She'd wait / until he nodded off, then put her foot down.' – My Mother, Driving) and again of his father ('you gave your life to coaches and Swarfega /...soon you had three sons / climbing trees and reading war comics' – Your most Unlikely Son). Again, there are references to uncertainty ('someone has kicked

the ladders away' – Sunday); to 'the dolphin of depression' (The Dolphin); also to love, as in this beautiful first stanza of 'The World of the Senses':

I yearn for this much-prized, painful love –
his smile, the way he moves his hips
when he cuts a loaf or stirs a soup
or my chest against his back – this love
that quietly lifts away when he falls asleep.

A very moving section, 'April Elegies', recalls the poet's Buddhist friend and colleague Mahananda: 'When I gave you your name you wept aloud' – Name-Giving). And this is precisely how *Yarn* takes off from *The Crumb Road*, because the poems here explore relationships simultaneously personal and Buddhist/religious, adult as well as adolescent.

At the book's core are two long dramatic monologues about encounters with the Buddha, where personal and religious stories coincide: 'The Cattle Farmer's Tale' and 'The Travellers from Orissa'. When I read the first aloud to my partner, a Japanese Zen Buddhist, he was captivated by its wonderful characterisations of the farmer Dhaniya and his wife, and of the Buddha himself. He loved the dramatic contrast of farming with spiritual work, the equivalent importance of looking after the paddy fields and looking after the 'fertile fields of the mind'. Only when both are taken care of can one say: 'If you want to rain, rain-god, then go ahead and rain!' The second poem is in the voice of Bhallika who with his brother Tapussa met the Buddha when they were young. The brothers react very differently to this meeting ('Tapussa's head was full of yarns') and Bhallika regrets that he did not follow the spiritual life:

I didn't follow the Blessed One that day.

I left with Tapussa, as I said, and walked
back into my life...
And though I'd loved my children...
I knew that day that I'd betrayed my life.

There is a third long poem, too, at the end
of the book: 'Aaron's Brother' is about an Eng-
lish mystic (rather than Moses? a note would
have been helpful), and again revolves around
siblings and their contrary experiences of the
divine/spiritual ('you must be proud / to have
a brother who speaks to God like that.')

For me, these long narrative poems are
delightfully full of incident, told in a decep-
tively calm blank verse, with surprising images
('as rare as hare's horn', 'you're the same age
as your nose / and just a few years older than
your teeth'). They tell 'implausible' (but never
unconvincing) 'yarns' that I did not know and
feel enriched by knowing. Yarn, too, in the sense
of a thread that runs through the texture of
the poems, a voice, colouring the other poems
about the poet's own family and relationships.

For my partner, the poems have an added
dimension of *satori*, the Japanese Zen word for
enlightenment, what Lucien Stryk in his intro-
duction to the poems of Shinkichi Takahashi
(*Triumph of the Sparrow*, Grove Press, 1986) calls
'the all-or-nothing striving after illumination'.
And he was thrilled to read Maitreyabandhu's
poem about the Japanese poet Ryōkan:

like walking in the evening
or bathing at the spring,
the moon already rising,
he preferred repeated things

('Ryōkan')

But what we both loved most is the story-telling,
even in a shorter poem like 'Asaṅga', the monk
who spent years meditating in a cave:

When Asaṅga came down from his mountain cave –
twelve years that had achieved nothing –
he saw a dog [...] with a suppurating sore that crawled
with maggots and blowflies. He knelt
and with his tongue he moved the maggots one by one

Yarn is an unusual, at times difficult, committed
and illuminating book.

Moved

Nichola Deane, *Trieste*
Smith/doorstop, £7.50

Lucille Gang Schulklapper, *Gloss*
Flarestack, £4.50

Paschalis Nikolaou, *12 Greek Poems
after Cavafy*, Shearsman, £6.50

Amy Evans, *Cont.*
Shearsman, £6.50

Damilola Odelola, *Lost & Found*
Eyewear, £5.00

Reviewed by Alison Brackenbury

O room for absence

open to the sky! [...]
          And if dust touches you
it sleeps in an eyelid bed, in half a world
singing lullay: *be here be whole be gone.*

These lines, from Nichola Deane's 'Bowl', reveal
a marvellously original writer of English poetry. I
can think of very few poets writing now who would
risk, and achieve, those final six words, light-
footed as song. Her fearless exclamations, which I
admire, suggest that she is also deeply moved by
the work of Rilke. In the title poem of her second
pamphlet, *Trieste*, 'Rilke's shade' speaks to 'the
sea wind [...] And weather, like a Spartan messen-
ger, / runs in, breathless'. There is no full stop.

Deane's poems move distinctively. Her lines
are often dense with alliteration, borne along
determinedly by internal rhymes. 'Fig Ghazal'
describes 'the women' 'with their force, drift,
thrift'. 'The poured-out song you hear' is 'muffled
on the other side of the locked door'. Lines which
might be narrowly personal move into a wider
world, of terrible repression.

I only have two reservations about this out-
standing second pamphlet. Deane can be drawn
to write by visual art, sometimes a dangerous
inspiration. Will phrases such as 'Rothko-black'
move readers who have not seen Rothko's paint-
ings? *Trieste* also includes one poem 'after lines
by Anne Carson', followed by another which
depends upon an (acknowledged) phrase from
Alice Oswald: 'unmasked light'. As a writer
and reader, I have many anxieties about both
kinds of poem. As, happily, Deane's use of them
is limited, I will confine myself to one brief
wail: 'There is Too Much of This Around!'

Let us move on, swiftly, to 'Yesterday's Child':

Sorrow and rage, rage and sorrow
are beads on a thread of ragged prayer

and yesterday's child can't cut the string
and her life is strung on thin thin air

she knowingly doggedly sowing tomorrow
with sorrow and rage and rage and sorrow.

Urgent metaphors, wild syntax, rugged rhyme, a
drumbeat of repetition – This story of the adult
trapped in the child's past is bitterly upsetting
and boldly true. Here is Nichola Deane at her
moving best.

'Imagine you're the youngest in a study group.
You're 79...' In her fifth chapbook, *Gloss*, Luci-
lle Gang Shulklapper proves exceptionally
good at introducing her own prose poems.
Her epigraph comes from Flannery O'Connor:
'*Where you come from is gone*'. Her contents

Some Contributors

Sam Adams edited *Poetry Wales* in the early 1970s and has been a contributor to *PN Review* since 1982.

Linda Anderson is the author of *Elizabeth Bishop: Lines of Connection* (EUP) and a poetry pamphlet from Mariscat, *Greenhouse*, both 2013. She is the Director of the Newcastle Centre for the Literary Arts at Newcastle University.

Ingeborg Bachmann (1926–1973) was an Austrian poet and author. Translated works include *Darkness Spoken: The Collected Poems of Ingeborg Bachmann*.

Alison Brackenbury's ninth collection of poems, *Skies*, was published by Carcanet in February 2016. New poems can be read on her website. alisonbrackenbury.co.uk

Vahni Capildeo is a British Trinidadian writer. *Simple Complex Shapes* (Shearsman, 2015) and *Measures of Expatriation* (Carcanet, 2016) are her most recent books.

John Clegg was born in Chester in 1986, and grew up in Cambridge. In 2013, he won an Eric Gregory Award. He works as a bookseller in London. *Holy Toledo!* will be published by Carcanet in May 2016.

Linda Goddard is Lecturer in Art History at the University of St Andrews. The featured essay first appeared in *The Institute Letter* for Fall 2015, published by the Institute for Advanced Study, Princeton.

David Herd is a poet, critic, teacher and activist. He is Professor of Modern Literature at the University of Kent and a co-organiser of Refugee Tales. His collections of poetry include *All Just* (Carcanet, 2012) and *Outwith* (Bookthug, 2012). *Through* will be published by Carcanet in 2016.

Eleanor Hooker is an Irish poet. She lives in North Tipperary. Her first collection, *The Shadow Owner's Companion* (The Dedalus Press), was published in 2012 and shortlisted for the Strong/Shine award for best first collection from that year. Her second collection, *A Tug of Blue*, will be published in 2016. www.eleanorhooker.com

Peter Hughes is the author of several collections of poetry, including a *Selected Poems* (Shearsman). His versions of Cavalcanty are forthcoming from Carcanet.

Eric Langley is a lecturer in Shakespeare at Royal Holloway, University of London. His book *Suicide and Narcissism in the Works of Shakespeare* was published by Oxford University Press in 2009.

Drew Milne's recent books of poetry include: *Burnt Laconics Bloom* (Oystercatcher, 2013); *the view from Royston cave* (Wide Range chapbooks, 2012) and *equipollence* (Song Cave, 2012). He is the Judith E Wilson Lecturer in Drama & Poetry, Faculty of English, University of Cambridge.

Stanley Moss was born in New York City in 1925. He makes his living as a private art dealer, largely in Spanish and Italian old masters, and is the publisher and editor of Sheep Meadow Press. *It's About Time*, his most recent collection of poems, was published by Carcanet in 2015.

Jamie Osborn founded Cambridge Student PEN, and is poetry editor at *The Missing Slate*. He is grateful for poetry conversations, and hopes to be confident and involved in Green politics.

Siriol Troup comes from a Welsh family but was born in Hong Kong and spent most of her childhood and teenage years abroad, in Africa, Germany, Holland and Iran. She read Modern Languages (French and German) at St Hugh's College, Oxford and later returned there to teach nineteenth- and twentieth-century French Literature.

Rebecca Watts was born in Suffolk in 1983 and lives in Cambridge. In 2014 she was one of the Poetry Trust's Aldeburgh Eight. *The Met Office Advises Caution*, her first collection, will be published by Carcanet in 2016.

David Wheatley is the author of *Contemporary British Poetry* (Palgrave, 2015). He lives in rural Aberdeenshire.

Editors
Michael Schmidt (General)
Luke Allan (Deputy)

Editorial address
The Editors at the address on the right. Manuscripts cannot be returned unless accompanied by a stamped self-addressed envelope or international reply coupon.

Trade distributors
Central Books Ltd
99 Wallis Road
London, E9 5LN
magazines@
centralbooks.com

Cover
Line, 2014
Hannah Devereux

Subscriptions (6 issues)
individuals: £39/$86
institutions: £49/$105
to: PN Review, Alliance House
30 Cross Street, Manchester
M2 7AQ, UK

Supported by

Type
Set in Arnhem Pro, Sentinel, and Averta by LA

Copyright
© 2016 Poetry Nation Review
all rights reserved
ISBN 978-1-78410-139-8
ISSN 0144-7076

Supported using public funding by
ARTS COUNCIL ENGLAND

list, headed 'Itinerary', lists the places where her poems journey: Italy, New York, Florida.

Shulklapper describes her peripatetic child-hood factually, without self-pity: 'Mother married Walter, who took the little money she used to hide'. Marriage takes her to 'the right address (though rats scurried)...' She can travel in imagination, surveying white nail varnish: 'polar bears swimming toward ice'. Some landmarks are unexpected. 'My desert rose' in Florida is an old man, 'twist-trunked'.

Gloss can be shockingly moving. A 'Widow at Cocktail Party' wonders 'if the knife is sharp enough to slit your wrists'. But the chapbook, although firmly structured, flares with fancies. Its 'Singles Dance' is populated by 'single canaries' and 'sneakered cats' 'watching the prince limp away on his rubber-tipped cane', as precision moves into kindly humour.

The poems dip from age into a sensuous past: 'Yes, she still thinks in Italian [...] Her language crunches cannoli sweetness'. 'Crunches' is typical of *Gloss*. The speaker savours, but is not over-whelmed. The writer is in control of the journey, sometimes maintaining careful distance. For the speaker in her last poem is a piece of glass, waiting 'to be made whole again by love'. I was left wondering, with warm interest, what will be Shulklapper's next destination in poetry.

12 Greek Poets after Cavafy is a little gem of a chapbook, described by its editor, Paschalis Nikolaou, as 'a kind of echo chamber within Greek letters'. He notes aspects of Cavafy's poetry probably unknown to non-Greeks, including 'his distinctive merging of the demotic and purist strands of the Greek language'. Yet he concludes that Cavafy's international appeal 'depends on a narrative drift'.

The chapbook contains twelve poems, in their original Greek and in English. The translations, by Nikolaou and Richard Berengarten, are clear, eloquent and beautifully unobtrusive. The poems are dated between 1916 and 2015: 'peaks within a very long chronicle'. I will pick out four high points. Timos Malanos offers his own striking story of Alexander, who, 'utterly fearlessly', drank a (possibly poisoned) medicine. In Angelos Parthenis's witty journey through time, Cavafy, concerned by floods of posthumous imitators, asks a living poet: 'Would you mind looking into the overall situation / and reporting back to me on this matter?' Yannis Ritsos, in 'The Poet's Space', creates an exquisite physical description of Cavafy, and 'the delicate reflections / of a sap-phire he wears on his finger'. In '16 March 2015, 6 p.m.', Dimitris Kosmopoulos records the death (probably suicide) of a young man persecuted by his peers. His final line may not address the boy, or Cavafy, but the reader: 'You know this, all of it. You know it all too well.' Its power is a tribute to Cavafy, to whose poems, surely, many readers of this chapbook will be moved to return.

After the rich density of notes and languages in the Cavafy anthology, it is a startling shift to the spacious pages of Amy Evans, often occupied only by a few words or symbols. The travelling reader might not realise that this chapbook is the third stop in a sequence. Evans splits words, by spacing or slashes, probing (and releasing) the meaning of each segment. The progress of each piece feels less like dissection than revelation: 'de live errs' (from a page headed **P.** [**T.**] **S.** [**D.**])

Reviewers can be guilty of passing through poems at reckless speed. Evans's work is the perfect corrective. Each line must be considered, unpicked. Her chapbook did not feel (to me) like a parlour game. Its care is underwritten by passion. She blends meanings with a rueful richness:

payn packet each month
record(s) losses: are you g/one? I

have lost

          my balance

I note, admiringly, that Evans's columns of words recall those of a balance sheet. These collages are clever – but never callous. There are quick lines whose devices verge on jokes, with subtly shaded spaces: 'hear t £s'. Others hold dark echoes of the world around us, and of desperate journeys. Evans's words may be airily spaced, but 'people / don't float / between / borders'. The pages of *Cont.* move from mathematical precision into music:

                              A long

accompanied song   for A   solo

                              voice

I will end with a brief appreciative note about Damilola Odelola's short but compelling first pam-phlet, dedicated to 'Brixton, pre hipster invasion'. (I am delighted to see that, since I drafted this review, *Lost & Found* has rightly become a Poetry Book Society Pamphlet Choice.)

Its first poem describes 'Those McDonald's boys'. Odelola has mastered simplicity, in the heraldic details of 'their uniform': 'And their black Air Force Ones, / And their silver chains'. But the 'McDonald's boys' are not marching through. They are defending territory in 'a war'. 'Their feet never move'.

The poems record shifts of names. 'Seun became Sean' (which his father hoped might secure 'a job in the city'). But Odelola's sequences are mirrors, reflecting different stages of a story: 'Sean returned to Seun [...] women / Like names that make you sing.' Her clear lines show that the movement of a life may be complicated, with wrong turn-ings: 'I've forgotten how to walk beside you.'

Odelola's powerfully patterned poetry can shift suddenly from repetition to change. The 'black gangs' have 'red blood'. Her final poem moves from the third to second person, as she speaks thoughtfully to 'The Boys Outside McDonald's'. Her poetry journeys back through time: 'Walk to Windrush Square'. But *Lost & Found* ends in the present, with colloquial lines which carry the authority of all that is lost before them. Her reader finds the full force of imagination: 'When you get back to that patch of concrete outside of McDonald's, / Remember that your feet were made to move.'